Sociology: A Very Short Introduction

Very Short Introductions available now:

For more information visit our web site
www.oup.co.uk/vsi

Steve Bruce

SOCIOLOGY

A Very Short Introduction

OXFORD
UNIVERSITY PRESS

Great Clarendon Street, Oxford OX2 6DP

Oxford University Press is a department of the University of Oxford.
It furthers the University's objective of excellence in research, scholarship,
and education by publishing worldwide in

Oxford New York

Athens Auckland Bangkok Bogotá Buenos Aires Calcutta
Cape Town Chennai Dar es Salaam Delhi Florence Hong Kong Istanbul
Karachi Kuala Lumpur Madrid Melbourne Mexico City Mumbai
Nairobi Paris São Paulo Shanghai Singapore Taipei Tokyo Toronto Warsaw

with associated companies in Berlin Ibadan

Oxford is a registered trade mark of Oxford University Press
in the UK and in certain other countries

Published in the United States
by Oxford University Press Inc., New York

British Library Cataloguing in Publication Data
Data available
ISBN 0-19-285380-5

7 9 10 8 6

Typeset by RefineCatch Ltd, Bungay, Suffolk
Printed in Spain by Book Print S. L.

Contents

Preface

It is a sign of the power of sociology that it is both popular and reviled. Longer established academic disciplines deride it as a gauche newcomer but adopt its perspectives. Ordinary people mock those who pursue it professionally, yet take some of its assumptions for granted. Governments accuse the discipline of undermining morality and social discipline, yet hire sociologists to evaluate their policies.

Our uneasiness with the discipline can be seen in the frequency and the nature of the jokes. This may just be my professional paranoia, but it seems that there are sociologist jokes in a way that there are not historian jokes. As such humour does not translate terribly well I will recount just one. This gem came from the British television series *Minder*, a fine 1980s comedy of minor villains and London low life. Two lovable rogues are discussing a mutual acquaintance who has just been released from prison. One announces that their friend has been improving himself while inside by studying: 'Yeh. He's got an Open University degree now. In sociology.' The second asks: 'Has he given up the thieving then?' and the first replies: 'Nah! But now he knows why he does it!'

This is a complex jibe: sociology appeals to villains (presumably because its focus is social problems); sociology, by showing the social causes of individual action, absolves people of responsibility; sociology is naïve and can be manipulated by the worldly-wise. Whether the discipline is guilty of any or all of these charges should be clear by the end of this short introduction.

For reasons that will become apparent, social scientists find it harder to agree than do natural scientists. Researchers at the leading edge of physics, for example, may argue ferociously, but there is sufficient consensus among the discipline's journeymen for an introductory physics textbook to state with authority the basic knowledge that is accepted by the trade. In contrast, introductory social science texts often describe their subjects as a series of competing perspectives. There are benefits to stressing what divides us. By taking specific emphases to their logical conclusions, we can readily perceive the arguments that need to be resolved if we are to explain this or that facet of the social world. Like politicians in elections, advocates of particular schools try to put 'clear blue water' between themselves and their rivals. But, like politicians in power, when the same advocates get round to doing sociology (rather than just advertising their brand of it) they tend to fall back to a common middle ground.

The narrow constraints of this 'Very Short Introduction' format free me from the obligation to map the discipline comprehensively. Instead I will try to convey the distinctive essence of the sociological vision. This will be done in three stages. First, I will explain the status of the enterprise by considering what is meant by describing sociology as a social science. In Chapters 2, 3, and 4 I will try to explain some of its fundamental assumptions. In the final chapter I will try to clarify the sociological enterprise by ridding it of some unfortunately popular impostors.

Acknowledgements

I would like to thank Professor Gordon Marshall of Nuffield College, Oxford, and George Miller of Oxford University Press for suggesting that I write this book. Professor Marshall, Professor Steven Yearley of the University of York, and Dr David Inglis of Aberdeen's Sociology Department, were kind enough to comment on early drafts. As always, Hilary Walford's copy-editing will have ensured that I have not said anything I did not mean to say.

Chapter 1
The Status of Sociology

Sociology and science

For as long as we have been impressed by our understanding and control of the material world, scientists and philosophers of science have tried to specify just what distinguishes successful modern science from such dead ends as trying to produce gold from stone or reading our future in the stars. Unfortunately all such attempts have failed to produce unambiguous lines of demarcation, and, when we have looked closely at what real scientists actually do, we often find that the working life of science fails to match the picture painted by the philosophers. None the less we can list a series of characteristics that are more likely to be found in astronomy than astrology, for example. While we cannot with absolute certainty divide ideas about the material world into science and pseudo-science, we can still profitably talk about things being 'more or less' scientific.

A good starting point is to assert that any good scientific theory should be internally consistent. This immediately separates it from much of what passes for lay reasoning. My mother contradicted herself more often than not. That something she said one moment was incompatible with her next pronouncement hardly ever troubled her. She once criticized a roadside café by asserting that the food was vile and the portions were too small!

A good scientific theory should accord with the evidence. This may seem obvious, but what the scientist should demand in this respect is considerably more rigorous than that which the lay person habitually accepts. Very different standards operate, for example, in conventional and in alternative medicine. Although driven by commercial imperatives to get their new wonder drugs to the market before those of their rivals, pharmaceutical companies subject their products to lengthy and extensive trials. In 'double-blind' testing, large numbers of patients are divided into test and control groups. One is given the new drug; the other a harmless and inert 'placebo'. Until the allocations are revealed at the end of the trials, neither patients nor doctors know who is getting the real drug and who the placebo. Only if the test sample shows a marked improvement over the placebo group is the trial accepted as good evidence of the effectiveness of the drug. In contrast, alternative therapies such as faith healing, acupuncture or magno-therapy are rarely tested; the personal experience of the practitioner, supported by a few anecdotes of miracle cures, is taken to be sufficient to establish effectiveness. Such testing as takes place is never double-blind, and thus the possibility that any perceived benefits result from a placebo effect is never eliminated.

Thirdly, science constantly changes. Its findings are never 'true' in an absolute now-and-forever sense; they are always provisional and can always be improved. The convincing orthodoxy of one century becomes the historical curiosity of the next. It is a little awkward to say that science makes *progress*, because we do not know where we are going, but we certainly know where we have been and can thus talk about science gradually moving away from error. Again we can see the point if we contrast the reliance of medical science on experimental proof with the reliance of alternative therapies on tradition. In the world of Bachian flower remedies, Feng Sui, and Shiatsu massage, that something has been done for centuries (preferably in a culture untainted by modernity) establishes its validity. Given that such fundamentals of medical science as the body's circulatory system are relatively recent discoveries, the scientist is rightly not impressed by the age of an idea.

In bad science (such as Erich Von Daniken's claims that the Egyptian pyramids were built by visiting spacemen) theories are supported by snippets of fact plucked out of context. In good science the key to the replacement of one explanation by another is the systematic collection of *extensive* data that bear on the matter.

But this is not enough. Few ideas are so bizarre that no evidence can be found to support them. Reasons to believe are quite easy to find. A much more telling test is to search for reasons not to believe, to seek evidence that does not fit. In good science the most persuasive ideas are those that survive repeated attempts to prove them wrong.

This brings us to one of the most important features of good science: the way it deals with failure. Imagine I develop a new theory about the behaviour of subatomic particles. In my laboratory, assisted by students whom I have trained in my perspective, I generate lots of experimental observations to fit my theory. But then scientists elsewhere repeat my work and fail to confirm my findings. I should reconsider my theory in the light of the new evidence. If it can be developed so as to encompass the new results or can explain why the new observations are misleading, then it stands. If not, we should abandon it.

The value of this approach is most easily seen if we consider an alternative. A client comes to a witch doctor with a very bad skin rash. The witch doctor poisons a chicken, and, from the way the chicken staggers before dropping dead, the witch doctor determines that the rash has been caused by the client's sister-in-law bewitching him. The client is given a charm and told that, if he wears it for a week, the spell will be broken and the rash will clear up. But it does not work: a month later the rash is as bad as ever. Instead of concluding that the idea that illness is caused by evil spells is nonsense and that the charm is without curative power, the witch doctor explains that the charm did not work because the client did not have enough faith. What appears to be failure is turned into further support for the system of belief.

Though this illustration is taken from African traditional medicine, we can find many examples of modern scientists being similarly inventive in trying to save their pet theories from refutation. Clearly good science would be served by scientists being very heavily committed to the scientific enterprise in general but not being overly attached to their own particular theories. But then scientists are only human. What saves the enterprise from having to depend on individual scientists being saintly in their detachment is the fact of *competition*. The person who has spent twenty years developing a particular theory about subatomic particles is likely to work hard to defend the body of ideas that has made his name. However, the career structure of natural science means that there will be lots of other people working in the same field who do not owe the great man any favours and who are desperately trying to prove him wrong in order to advance their own competing explanations.

Science thrives on the free exchange of ideas and on intellectual competition. It stagnates when, as happened in the Middle Ages under the Catholic Church and under Stalin in the Soviet Union, an outside agency tries to impose on scientists an orthodoxy that is not rooted in the work of the discipline. In the nineteenth century some geneticists argued that characteristics that individuals acquired during their lifetimes could be passed on through their genes. French biologist J.-B. Lamarck believed that the giraffe owed its long neck to the habit of stretching to feed on tree leaves. The counter-case would suppose that 'long-necked-ness' was already a genetically encoded quality and that those giraffes that possessed it had a better chance of survival than those that did not. So genetic stock changes through 'natural selection' rather than learning. By the 1920s the Lamarckian view had been largely abandoned. However, it survived in the Soviet Union, where the natural-selection alternative was thought to be too close to the logic of capitalism and hence politically unacceptable. T. D. Lysenko used his political position to have Lamarckism incorporated in official Communist philosophy, and those geneticists who opposed him were either forced to recant or exiled to Siberia. Only in the 1950s did Soviet biology recover from Lysenko's influence. Sadly, the official sponsorship of the wrong side of the argument blighted not only Soviet biology but also the Soviet economy. The ideologically justified rejection of 'bourgeois' genetics cut the Soviet Union's agriculture off from the great advances in crop development enjoyed in the West.

It is now fashionable to deride the idea that the scientific method guarantees truth. Sociology has itself played a significant part in undermining the grander claims of science by showing that its ways of working are often similar to the mundane methods ordinary people use to make sense of the world and that scientists are not immune to interests and values that compromise their claims to detachment. None the less, modern science has been so successful in allowing us to understand and manipulate the natural world (far too successful, many critics would say) that it offers an obvious place to start when we consider how we might study the social world. That is, it is not an accident that, in most university structures, sociology is to be found, not with 'arts and humanities', but in faculties of 'social science'.

Can sociology be scientific?

However, if we begin our description of the sociological enterprise by saying that it should model itself on the methods of the physical sciences, we cannot proceed very far before recognizing some fundamental limits to such imitation.

The first is that social scientists can rarely construct experiments. While researching the Ulster Defence Association (UDA) and the Ulster Volunteer Force (UVF), the two main loyalist terrorist organizations in Northern Ireland, I became interested in how certain people had come to occupy important leadership roles. Having found out everything I could about the leaders (and about those who might have been regarded as leadership material but never made it), I came to a number of tentative conclusions. Contrary to what one might expect of terrorist organizations, it was not personal viciousness that kept leaders in office. Out of some thirty cases, I could find only two people who had ruled by fear. One of them was murdered by his own people as soon as his more senior protectors had lost office; the other would have been had he not been arrested and imprisoned. What was much more important than naked coercion was the talent of being able to persuade and reconcile. However, this skill seemed to be common among UDA and UVF leaders across the twenty-five years of the organization, which left unexplained a major difference in the background of those who commanded the UDA and UVF in the 1970s and those who replaced them in the mid-1980s.

While diplomacy was a general requirement, social status was important for the first decade but not thereafter. The first generation of leaders were almost always people who had occupied some sort of community leadership role *before* the Troubles broke out and the Protestants of working-class areas started to organize themselves into vigilante groups. They had held office in trade unions, community associations, the Ulster Unionist party, and housing associations. The men who came to prominence in the late 1980s were very different. Most had grown up in the terrorist organizations and had come to the fore because they were 'operators' – ruthless killers and planners of terrorist actions or of such necessary subsidiary activities as fund-raising by bank-robbing, extortion, and drug-dealing.

The differences between the generations led me to the following conclusion. In a new enterprise, where no one has experience or can point to a track-record, general marks of status or competence are called on to determine leadership. In modern educational jargon, leadership is taken to be a transferable skill. But once an enterprise has been going for long enough for large numbers to have gained experience of its core activities (in this case, planning or carrying out murders and related criminal acts), then it becomes possible to judge potential candidates for leadership on the core skills of the organization.

So the attention of members shifts from very general marks of competence (such as having been prominent in some other community activity) to more specific task-related attributes.

This explanation could be quite wrong. What matters for my purposes here is how I could further test my idea. The chemist studying bromide reactions could have devised further experiments that held constant what were taken to be extraneous variables and focused changes on just those things that were thought to be central. But I could not, for experimental purposes, take a previously stable society and start a minor civil war. No reader should need persuading that the pursuit of social-scientific knowledge cannot justify terrorism. Even if I had had no ethical scruples, it would have been impractical. I had neither the wealth nor the power to start a small war and motivate people to take part in it.

However, let us imagine that both ethical and practical obstacles had been overcome. Creating my own terror group would still not have produced data comparable to those from the repeated experiments of the bromide chemist, because my terror group would not have been the same as the 'naturally occurring' ones I wished to understand. There are two problems. One is that artificial experiments in the social sciences have a fundamentally different relationship to the real world than chemistry experiments because the social experiment is not a facsimile of the naturally occurring: it is itself a novel social event. The other issue is that social life appears to be too complex to be broken down into simple component parts that can then be examined in isolation.

So one major difference between the natural and social sciences is that the ideas of the latter cannot normally be rigorously tested by being subjected to experiments that isolate the features of human action that interest us from the complexities of ongoing life. However, we can and often do perform quasi-experiments in which we try to compare the action that interests us in a variety of settings that are mostly similar but different in just one or two key ways. The work of Rosabeth Kanter on utopian communities provides a good illustration. She wanted to know why some communes succeeded while others failed. Her extensive reading of the history of such groups and her own involvement in the communes of the 1960s had given her some general ideas about which features of such engineered societies might work. So she began with some hypotheses, derived from previous scholarly work and shaped by her own unsystematic observation, and then sought a test of those ideas. To avoid the effects of differences in the communities being swamped by differences in their surrounding societies, she concentrated on communes that had been formed in one country within a relatively short time period: the United States between 1780 and 1860. She managed to identify ninety such communities: eleven 'successes' that had survived twenty-five years (the conventional view of a generation) and seventy-nine 'failures' that had not lasted a quarter of a century. She concluded that, although there was no short list of properties that were present in all the successes and uniformly absent from the failures, there were characteristics that were common in almost all of the communities that had survived one generation and were rare in the failures. The successes demanded various forms of sacrifice (such as abstinence from sex, alcohol, and dancing) from their members. They had world-views that drew hard lines between the good people of the commune and the rest of the world. They had very strict definitions of membership and rigorous membership tests. New members were required to prove their commitment by investing a great deal of time and money in the enterprise, which in turn made it costly to defect. Almost all the successes bolstered this psychic and social separation from the world with geographical isolation. Kanter concluded that commitment was not a mysterious phenomenon that had to precede the formation of a utopian community. Rather it was a social property that could be engineered by the deliberate use of what she called 'commitment mechanisms'.

Researchers since have modified Kanter's conclusions. I have argued that it is easier to engineer commitment to some sorts of belief-systems than to others. Those political philosophies and religions that vest supreme authority in the individual are far more difficult to organize than those that can evoke some higher power. Conservative Catholics and Protestants can form successful communities; liberal Protestants and devotees of the New Age cannot. However, here I am more interested in Kanter's method than in her conclusions. She very ably demonstrates that, while we cannot experiment as easily as the natural scientist, with some imagination we can find 'naturally occurring' data, examples from real life, to simplify social phenomena.

Social scientists routinely do this with large-scale social surveys. Imagine we want to know what effect gender has on political preferences. We could ask large numbers of men and women how they voted in the 1997 election that brought Labour to power in Britain after eighteen years of Conservative rule, and compare the answers. However, if we stopped there we would learn very little, because other characteristics such as income, levels of education, race, and religion also affect political preferences. So we would ask our men and women further questions that allowed us to assign them labels for levels of income, years in formal education, ethnic identity, religious affiliation, and so on. We could then use statistical methods to work out which of these characteristics, either on its own or in combination, has the greatest effect on voting behaviour.

While such research is illuminating, its conclusions are always tentative and probabilistic. We can say with confidence that working-class people are more likely to lean to the left politically than the upper classes. But there are enough exceptions to that proposition to stop us treating it as if it were a natural law. In the 1950s it was possible to identify a group of 'deferential workers' that, though we might want to call it 'objectively' working class, was none the less extremely conservative in its politics and supposed that the upper classes would make a better job of running the country than the representatives of the workers. In the 1980s

Margaret Thatcher's brand of conservatism (*laissez-faire* on economics but authoritarian on social issues) drew strong support from sections of the working class in the prosperous south-east of England. So we start with a simple expectation and find that it needs to be refined. Simple divisions of people by type of occupation (such as manual and non-manual work) are not powerful predictors of voting. So we further divide class or we add other considerations, but we find that our propositions never move beyond probabilities.

Some sociologists take such failures as encouragement to become more sophisticated in the definition, identification, and measurement of what are taken to be the causes of social action. While improvement in those three areas is all to the good, sociology's failure to produce 'laws' reflects far more than its relative immaturity. After a century of scientific sociology, the 'it's-early-days-yet' defence sounds rather thin. More research and more sophisticated methods of analysing the data we collect will make us better informed, but we will never discover the laws of human action because people are not like atoms.

The subject matter of the social sciences is conscious sentient beings who act out of choice. At this stage we do not need to get bogged down in well-rehearsed arguments about the extent to which people are really 'free'. All we have to recognize is that, whatever the sources of uniformity in human behaviour (and more of that later), they are not 'binding' in any absolute sense. The most oppressive regime may constrain us so tightly that we can choose only between conformity and death, but we can still choose the latter. This distinguishes us utterly from the subject matter of the natural sciences. Water cannot refuse to have its volatility increased as it is heated. With pressure held constant, water cannot boil at 100°C for four days and then refuse to do so on the fifth day. People can. Even the lowest worm can turn.

This leads us to recognize that what counts as explanation in the social sciences is quite unlike explanation in physics or chemistry. We explain why the kettle boils by citing the general laws of pressure, temperature, and volatility. Because the water has not *decided* to boil (a decision that it could change on some other occasion), we do not need to refer to the consciousness of the water. If we wish only to identify some very broad regularities of human behaviour, then we can treat social characteristics like the variables of natural science and propose, for example, that unskilled workers are more likely than businessmen to vote socialist, but if we wish to *explain* why that is the case then we have to examine the beliefs, values, motives, and intentions of the people in question. Because the human consciousness is the engine that drives all action, the social sciences have to go further than the natural sciences. When the chemist has repeatedly found the same reactions in his bromides, he stops. Identifying the regularity is the end of that search. For the social scientist it is only the beginning. Even if we found that everyone in a particular situation always did a particular thing (and such strong regularities are almost unknown), we would want to know *why*.

The words 'what' and 'why' can neatly express the difference. For the chemist they can be the same thing. When you have collected enough data under the right controlled circumstances to be confident you know what happens, you also know why. But when the German sociologist Max Weber collected enough information to persuade himself that there was some strong connection between the spread of the Puritan branch of the Protestant Reformation and the rise of modern industrial capitalism (the 'what' issue), he had only begun. He wanted to know *why* the Puritans developed a set of attitudes that were particularly conducive to modern entrepreneurial methods. He wanted to know why a particular set of religious beliefs could have created a novel attitude to work and to consumption. He sought the answer in the minds of the Puritans. In order to explain, he had to understand.

The sociologist's interest in beliefs, values, motives, and intentions brings with it concerns unknown in the natural sciences. In order to understand people, we need to solicit their views or 'accounts' of what they are doing. Furthermore, we can take the same point back one step and note that it is not just understanding that requires some interest in motives. Even *identifying* the social act we wish to understand requires attention to motives. Let us go back to our pan of water. There are ways of defining when a liquid changes to a gas that make no reference to its state of mind. But the actions of people cannot be identified simply by observing them. Or, to put it another way, the action itself is not enough. Suppose we are interested in how people interact in public places. We could sit at a table in a crowded railway station and watch and take notes. But if we confined ourselves only to what was visible, we would learn little. We could note 'man facing platform raises arm in air and moves it from side to side'. We could not say 'man waves to greet incoming passenger', because that second description gives a particular interpretation to the physical action. He might actually be trying to relieve a trapped nerve.

For very simple acts performed by people of our own culture, we can often assume we know their significance. I have met enough people off trains to know 'waving' when I see it. But suppose the action involved kneeling and lowering and raising the body with the arms outstretched. If it was Peking, it might be a form of exercise. If it was Cairo, it might be a Muslim at prayer. In the end the only way to ascertain the meaning of the action is (in some way or another) to ask the person in question: 'What are you doing?' So even the identification of actions requires some attention to motives and intentions.

Even more so does the explanation of actions. In one way or another the sociologist ends up having to ask people 'why are you doing this?'. But the very fact of asking (in whatever form) is itself a piece of social interaction. The accounts that people give can be both honest attempts to reconstruct past motives and performances through which they pursue present interests.

In some settings the distortion is obvious. We can be sure that the story people give of their actions during their defence in court, or in pleading for mitigation after admitting guilt, will be quite different from the version they give to friends and family after they have been found 'Not guilty' or avoided a custodial sentence. The person telling the story has interests in the outcome of the telling and the court itself requires stories to be told in an unusually stylized manner. I am not saying that the formal courtroom version is false and the informal version true. What I am saying is that giving an account is itself a social activity and not merely an explanation of earlier activities.

Another example can be drawn from religious conversion stories. It is common in evangelical Protestant circles for converts to 'witness' to their faith by recounting their experience of conversion. One need hear only a very small number of these testimonies to realize that they follow a few common templates. The convert was raised in the faith by a godly mother who did her best to keep the child on the straight and narrow, but the temptations of the world were too great, and the child fell away into a life of sin. Whatever pleasures that life produced turned to ashes in the mouth. Some precipitating crisis (often the death of the saintly mother or another loved one) brought the convert 'under conviction of sin'. 'As I drove home that night, I felt a weight of sin pressing on me. I realized that if I died then I was going to hell. I stopped the car and prayed for Jesus to come into my life.' The day and the time and the place are stated. In the final paragraph of the story, the convert relates how much his life has changed for the better since he gave himself to the Lord. Now, it may be that such testimonies are very similar because the underlying reality they purport to describe is similar. But, given that anyone raised in an evangelical culture will have heard hundreds of such stories, it is always possible that the similarities stem from the popularity of the story form and its role in shaping how people interpret their experiences.

I repeatedly encountered a version of this problem in my interviews with loyalist paramilitaries in Northern Ireland. Some people, probably from reticence well ingrained from years of resisting police interrogation, deliberately downplayed their role in terrorist crimes. Others, presumably to 'put the wind up' a middle-class academic, exaggerated their crimes. One man was so keen to brag of his deeds that he claimed a murder I knew he had not committed. When I mentioned this to another loyalist, he dismissively said: 'Aye, that's Judge Dread for you. He'd claim he topped Bambi's Mum if you asked him.' But the problem of the research interview itself distorting the evidence it seeks to collect is not confined to research on crime and other obviously sensitive subjects. It pervades every kind of social investigation, because the act of investigation introduces new variables.

To give just one example, public-opinion pollsters used to ask people how they felt about this or that and report their answers without considering that the very fact of asking people might lead them to assert feelings about things of which they knew nothing and cared even less. One Californian survey slipped in a question about an entirely fictitious issue that was supposedly to appear on a forthcoming referendum. Respondents were asked 'You will have heard of the Snibbo amendment. How do you feel about it?' and they were given the options of 'strongly support', 'support', 'am neutral', 'disapprove', and 'strongly disapprove'. A large proportion of respondents claimed to be either in favour or against, many of them strongly so. Perhaps they felt they would look foolish if they admitted they had no idea what the interviewer was talking about. Perhaps they were just trying to be helpful. Perhaps the nature of the interaction ('Here I am answering questions') led respondents to get so firmly into the way of giving definite responses that inertia carried them over what they should have seen as a break in the tracks.

What people say and what they actually did might be linked in four ways. First, respondents may not recall or understand their motives. Secondly, they may recall or understand all too well but deliberately dissemble. The nineteenth-century industrialist J. P. Morgan hit on an important point about the desire to appear decent and honourable when he said: 'For every act there are two reasons: a good reason and the real reason.' Thirdly, whatever the level of self-understanding and willingness to be honest, the setting for the giving of accounts may exert such an influence that we cannot with confidence use what people say as a guide to their previous mental states. Individual variety might be funnelled into apparent consensus: the conversion testimony is an example. Between these last two types, we can place a fourth case: collective dissembling. Often a group of people share what for them are good reasons for their actions but routinely 'explain' what they do by calling on a publicly more acceptable language of justification. For example, doctors may ration expensive treatments for renal failure or lung cancer by informal moralizing about what sort of person *deserves* their attention, but then avoid having to defend such reasoning by claiming that decisions were made solely on grounds of the likelihood of the intervention being successful.

One possible response to the variable relationship between why people act and what they later say about their actions is to give up trying to understand what Harold Garfinkel disparaged as 'what goes on in people's heads'. The more radical of Garfinkel's students argued that we cannot in the conventional sense *understand* people. All we can do is study the mechanics of account-giving. Thus we can analyse the formal structures of courtroom talk but we cannot use that talk to determine guilt. We can describe religious conversion testimonies in the same way that we can analyse an orchestral score, but we cannot use them as data to explain conversion.

This is an unwarranted conclusion. There are no magical spells that, if correctly performed, will separate the information that leads us to understand from the dross that deflects our attention. But, equally well, courts sometimes arrive at the truth; skilful interrogators penetrate obfuscatory defences; pollsters find ways of overcoming 'compliance effects'; and industrious researchers get a fix on an obscured area of social activity by studying it from a variety of angles. That we have no infallible technique does not mean that we are bound always to fail. If ordinary people can sometimes draw warranted conclusions from speech, why not the social scientist?

So far the differences between the natural and social sciences have been discussed to the disadvantage of the latter. I would now like to suggest a very different conclusion. Consider the position of racehorse trainers. Long experience may give them confidence that they can put themselves in the horses' hooves. But social scientists begin with the great advantage of sharing biology, psychology, and a great deal of culture with their subjects. I have never been a member of a terrorist organization and I have oriented my life around avoiding assassination and arrest. But I can find in my own experience causes to which I have been strongly attached, events that have caused me great fear and anger, and actions of which I am proud and others of which I am profoundly ashamed. Even when those we study seem as distant as citizens of a foreign country, there is enough in our common humanity to create countless border-crossings. We may misunderstand, but there will be opportunities to clear up confusion. Whatever analytical purchase is lost by us not being able to experiment is amply regained by our ability to sustain extended conversations with our subjects. I could not test my ideas about terrorist career structures experimentally, but I could, directly and indirectly, raise them with my respondents.

Conclusion

To summarize, whatever reservations we may have about how closely actual scientists conform to the high standards set in their programmatic statements about what they do and why it works, we need not doubt that the natural sciences offer the best available template for acquiring knowledge about the material world. Critical reasoning, honest and diligent accumulation of evidence, subjecting ideas to test for internal consistency and for fit with the best available

Sociology

evidence, seeking evidence that refutes rather than supports an argument, engaging in open exchanges of ideas and data unconstrained by ideological commitments: all of these can be profitably adopted by the social sciences. However, we need to appreciate the differences between the subject matter of the natural and the human sciences. People think. They act as they do, not because they are bound to follow unvarying rules but because they have beliefs, values, interests, and intentions. That simple fact means that, while some forms of sociological research look rather like the work of chemists or physicists, for the sociologist there is always a further step to take. Our notion of explanation does not stop at identifying regular patterns in social action. It requires that we understand.

Chapter 2
Social Constructions

Defining sociology

Most disciplines can be described either by the focus of their attention or by their basic assumptions. Thus we could say that economists study the economy or we could say that economists assume that a fundamental principle of human behaviour is the desire to 'maximize'. If we can buy an identical product in two shops at two different prices, we will buy the cheaper one. From that simple assumption an increasingly complex web of assumptions is spun. For example, economists go on to assume that, as the price of wheat falls, so demand for it will increase. As the price of wheat goes up, so farmers will produce more.

Similarly we could describe sociology as the study of social structures and social institutions, and sociological work is often divided into such topics as the class structure of modern societies, the family, crime and deviance, religion, and so on. However, to list what we study gives no sense of what is distinctive about the way we do it. Like a charm bracelet, this account of sociology will hang a number of substantial observations from a central thread made of the following strands: reality is socially constructed, our behaviour has hidden social causes, and much of social life is profoundly ironic.

Humans create culture

When Darwin's theory of evolution seeped into popular culture, it became common to see humans as just big clever animals. At the start of the twentieth century the notion of instincts provided a popular way of explaining our actions. At the end of the century, advances in mapping genes allow us to explain certain sorts of illness and the idea that we were determined by our biology has again become popular.

An easy way to dismiss the more extreme forms of biological determinism is to point to the many ways we deliberately reject instincts. There may be a will to live but we can commit suicide. There may be a will to reproduce, but women can choose not to have children and still live apparently fulfilled lives. There may be a sex urge, but celibacy is possible. The claims for biology are further weakened if we note the considerable cultural differences in what might be instinctual. Not only do people kill themselves but the suicide rate differs from one society to another, as does the frequency of childlessness. Whatever part instinct plays in our lives, it is complicated by cultural variations.

Yet biology can provide a useful starting point because, if we understand the extent to which the biology of lower animals determines their lives, and then appreciate the extent to which it *fails* to do so for humans, we can see the tremendous importance of culture. Ants do not ponder whether to follow the lead ant. They follow each other because their genes programme them so to do. Salmon do not consider where might be nice to reproduce; they automatically return to spawn where they spawned before. In contrast, humans derive very little direction from their biology, which creates difficulties: for the individual in terms of self-management and for the group in terms of coordination. As I will explain below, what follows is thoroughly artificial in that it poses problems we have already solved. None the less, by understanding those problems, we can appreciate the importance of the solutions.

Arnold Gehlen used the term 'world-openness' when he contrasted the enormous potential of the human condition with the very limited opportunities enjoyed by other animals. Our practical capabilities far outstrip those of other species. Bulls can eat, walk, and run around, bang heads with other bulls, and mount those cows that are in heat. And that is about it. Bulls cannot transcend the constraints of their environment. We can build towns under the Alaskan ice where those who work extracting oil from the frozen wastes can enjoy a Jacuzzi and watch Hollywood films in a heated cinema. There is so much we *could* do that, without some guidelines as to what we *should* do, we would be paralysed by indecision. So we simplify by creating routines and forming habits. What worked one day becomes the template for action the next. We get up about the same time every day, eat the same sorts of things, and put on the same sort of clothes. By ignoring most of our possibilities and treating a large part of the rest as habits, we retain just a small area of the world for freely chosen thought-about actions.

But, even once habit-forming has reduced world-openness to something manageable, we would still be ruined by the inherent restlessness identified by French sociologist Émile Durkheim. He begins with the proposition that 'No living being can be happy or even exist unless his needs are sufficiently proportioned to his means'. For most other animals, such equilibrium is established 'with automatic spontaneity'. The goals of the ant are simple and are determined by its biology. The extent to which it can meet those goals is determined by its environment. The ant is satisfied or it is dead. It makes no sense to talk of an unhappy or alienated or frustrated ant. As Durkheim puts it:

> When the void created by existence in its own resources is filled, the animal, satisfied, asks nothing further. Its power of reflection is not sufficiently developed to imagine other ends than those implicit in its physical nature. . . . This is not the case with man, because most of his needs are not dependent on his body or not to the same degree.

Consider the consequences of our freedom from instinctual or environmental control. No matter how much we achieve or acquire, we can always want to have or have been more. Indeed success seems only to stimulate further desire. The young man wants a car. After much saving, he acquires a Citroen 2CV. For a year or so, he is content. Then he begins to resent being overtaken by everything else on the road and yearns for a car with four cylinders. With further saving, he progresses to a Vauxhall Viva, which is faster than the 2CV, and, for a year or so, he is a happy motorist. But then he wants a car with a powerful engine and the yearning returns. So he graduates to a Vauxhall Cavalier. And so it goes. Even when he buys the car of his dreams, he can want two cars: the powerful saloon for motorways and a four-wheel-drive vehicle for the rough countryside around his house.

In part such frustration is a modern problem, a consequence of the weakening of the traditional restraints. In part it is a direct result of capitalist advertising stimulating the desires. But the problem is also a general one. What Durkheim wrote at the start of the twentieth century could refer to non-material goals as much as to material possessions.

> All man's pleasure in acting, moving and exerting himself implies the sense that his efforts are not in vain and that by walking he has advanced. However, one cannot advance when one walks toward no goal, or – which is the same thing – when his goal is infinity. Since the distance between us and it is always the same, whatever road we take, we might as well have made the motions without progress from the spot. Even our glances behind and our feelings of pride at the distance covered can cause only deceptive satisfaction, since the remaining distance is not proportionately reduced. To pursue a goal which is by definition unattainable is to condemn oneself to perpetual unhappiness.

The solution is *regulation*. A moral force, a shared culture that specifies what we can desire and how we can attain those goals, takes the place of the biological straitjacket. To fill the gap left by what Gehlen called 'instinctual deprivation', people create social frameworks. Some parts of those frameworks may be fixed in formal law. The bulk of it is merely conventional. There is no law that says that white-collar workers in management positions should wear dark two-piece suits, but every aspirant to senior management knows how to dress. At its most effective, the straitjacket is applied not to the outside of the body but to the inside of the mind. We are socialized in the culture so that important elements of it become embedded in our personalities.

If we can see the importance of culture in giving a framework within which the individual can achieve contentment, the third problem of world-openness – coordinating joint action – should be even more obvious. Where, as with ants and bees, communication and coordination are themselves biological, there is no difficulty. One ant does not need to interpret the signals given off by another. It responds automatically to the secretions. Even complex matters such as arranging the appropriate combinations of roles within a hive of bees are not debated by the bees. They respond automatically to the death of the queen bee by feeding another egg the genetic material which will turn it into a queen.

Roles

Human biology does nothing to structure human society. Age may enfeeble us all, but cultures vary considerably in the prestige and power they accord to the elderly. Giving birth is a necessary condition for being a mother, but it is not sufficient. We expect mothers to behave in maternal ways and to display appropriately maternal sentiments. We prescribe a clutch of norms or rules that govern the *role* of mother. That the social role is independent of the biological base can be demonstrated by going back three sentences. Giving birth is certainly not sufficient to be a mother but, as adoption and fostering show, it is not even necessary!

The fine detail of what is expected of a mother or a father or a dutiful son differs from culture to culture, but everywhere behaviour is coordinated by the *reciprocal* nature of roles. Husbands and wives, parents and children, employers and employees, waiters and customers, teachers and pupils, warlord and followers; each makes sense only in its relation to the other. The term 'role' is an appropriate one, because the metaphor of an actor in a play neatly expresses the rule-governed nature or scripted nature of much of social life and the sense that society is a joint production. Social life occurs only because people play their parts (and that is as true for wars and conflict as for peace and love) and those parts make sense only in the context of the overall show. The drama metaphor also reminds us of the artistic licence available to the players. We can play a part straight or, as the following from J.-P. Sartre conveys, we can ham it up.

> Let us consider this waiter in the café. His movement is quick and forward, a little too precise, a little too rapid. He comes towards the patrons with a step a little too quick. He bends forward a little too eagerly; his voice, his eyes express an interest a little too solicitous for the order of the customer. Finally there he returns, trying to imitate in his walk the inflexible stiffness of some kind of automaton while carrying his tray with the recklessness of a tightrope-walker. . . . All his behaviour seems to us a game. . . . But what is he playing? We need not watch long before we can explain it: he is playing at being a waiter in a café.

The American sociologist Erving Goffman built an influential body of social analysis on elaborations of the metaphor of social life as drama. Perhaps his most telling point was that it is only through acting out a part that we express character. It is not enough to be evil or virtuous; we have to be seen to be evil or virtuous.

The distinction between the roles we play and some underlying self will be pursued later. Here we might note that some roles are more absorbing than others. We would not be surprised by the waitress who plays the part in such a way as to signal to us that she is much more than her occupation. We would be surprised and offended by the father who played his part 'tongue in cheek'. Some roles are broader and more far-reaching than others. Describing someone as a clergyman or faith healer would say far more about that person than describing someone as a bus driver. Here the main point I want to make is that, in the absence of strong biological linkages, reciprocal roles provide the mechanism for coordinating human behaviour.

Order and orders

To prevent my line of argument from becoming confused with a related point, I would like to add a brief aside. Durkheim and Gehlen are often misunderstood by being narrowly depicted as political conservatives. To see only their concern with political stability is to miss the bigger point. All human action, conservative or radical, reactionary or revolutionary, requires some basic ordering. Thomas Hobbes worried that without some external power imposing civility, people would selfishly pursue their own interests to the detriment of the good of all. My point is that even such self-seeking requires a considerable amount of common culture. Even anarchists must stabilize their characters, communicate with each other, and understand the enemy!

We make life manageable by creating social institutions that do for us what instincts do for other animals. By routinizing programmes of action and either painting them onto the 'backcloth' or writing them into a script, we can leave free for creative improvisation and conscious choice an area that is small enough for individuals and groups to manage without becoming overwhelmed.

However, though we may on calm reflection see the virtues of allowing large parts of our lives to follow well-worn paths, modern people periodically feel themselves frustrated by the impersonality and predictability of life. As Laurie Taylor and Stan Cohen illustrate in *Escape*

Attempts, we often try to distinguish between the social roles we play and the real 'us'. Like Sartre's waiter, we perform in such a way as to show to our audiences that we are more than, and can rise above, our roles as managers, civil servants, bus drivers, fathers, and loyal spouses. We may use hobbies, holidays, and weekend trips to establish a persona separate from our place in the paramount reality of everyday life. However, and this reinforces Gehlen's case for the importance of shared order, even these escape attempts are commonplace and repetitious. Just as sheep without thinking about it will take the same least arduous route around a hill, so, even when we think we are engaging in daring, radical, and convention-defying acts, our lives tend to follow well-beaten tracks. The middle-aged businessman, bored with his wife and family, tries to rediscover his autonomy (and his youth) by having a fling with his secretary. He imagines he is an explorer heading out into uncharted waters, but, in his attempt to escape from the oppressive routines of his daily life, he merely embraces yet another well-worked script. He has climbed over the prison wall to what, for a while, he imagines is freedom, but he soon concludes that he has simply fallen into the exercise yard of a different prison.

The solidity of culture

The above is one development of the idea that reality is socially constructed. Against those who suppose that the regularities in human action stem from our common biology, the sociological perspective begins by noting that humans differ from other animals in the extent to which their worlds are open and potentially unformed. Hence such regularities as we find (and we find them often because they are essential to the maintenance of psychic and social stability) are a product of culture: people make it up. And culture cannot be reduced to biology.

There is a further small but important version of this claim. Even when objective stimuli are implicated in our actions, it is our *interpretations* of those stimuli that affect our behaviour. Consider the way we 'get drunk'. It is unlikely that there are major differences in the way that the Australian Aboriginal farmer, the New York businessman, the Scottish medical student, and the Italian child metabolize alcohol, but there are huge variations in how these peoples behave when they drink. I do not mean just that cultures differ in attitudes to drunkenness, though they do. What is acceptable for a fishing crew returned from a week in the north Atlantic is not what one would expect at a business lunch in Tokyo. I mean that the 'overlay' of culture is such that different peoples *expect* alcohol to affect them in different ways and as a result do indeed feel different. The amount of alcohol that in one context produces staggering, incoherent speech, and incontinent giggling can in another produce quiet reflection and feelings of peace. Or, to put it another way, we learn what to expect and by and large find it. As Howard Becker argued in his seminal essay 'Becoming a Marijuana User', the same objective sensation could be interpreted as elation or nausea and learning to feel the former rather than the latter is a crucial part of becoming a dope smoker.

This brings me to an aspect of sociology that causes great difficulty for novices. It is tempting to divide the world into things that are real and things that are imagined: an objective external reality and subjective internal landscapes. One of my students, who lacked both a way with words and a sense of the ridiculous, managed to summarize criticisms of biological explanations of schizophrenia by saying 'So we can see that mental illness is all in the mind'! Possibly, but the realm that interests sociologists is neither 'all in the mind' nor entirely external to our consciousness: it is inter-subjective. Things that people imagine, provided they are imagined similarly by large enough numbers of people, can have an enduring and even oppressive reality indistinguishable from the 'objective' world. In considering how we explain our actions, the American social psychologist W. I. Thomas wrote that, if people define situations as real, then they are real in their consequences. The man who believes his house is on fire will run from it.

That the house does not burn down proves his belief was wrong, but none the less, to understand why the man evacuates his house what matters is his belief and not the 'truth'.

The same point can be made on a much bigger scale if we consider a social institution such as religion. Sociologists do not want to get involved in the tricky business of deciding which religion, if any, is correct. We need observe only that there are hundreds of religions, many of which are basically incompatible. If Roman Catholics are right, then evangelical Protestants, Muslims, Hindus, and Buddhists are wrong. So we can accept minimally that one or more religion is mistaken. Yet religious belief systems can be immensely powerful. The Christian Church in the Middle Ages exercised enormous power. It ruled states and its beliefs shaped high culture and the everyday lives of the people. Through its rituals, and the ideas expressed in those rituals, the Church provided an accompaniment to birth, marriage, and death and to the cycle of changing seasons. Although detailed theological knowledge was restricted to the few people who were literate, almost everyone knew that there was a God who had made the earth and heaven and hell, who demanded certain types of behaviour, and who punished and rewarded. Even the not-especially devout shaped their behaviour to conform to the Church's interpretation of divine requirements and had frequent recourse to the Church's magic. Blessed amulets, holy water, relics of the saints, and a forest's worth of pieces of the Holy Cross were objects of veneration and practical devices to improve health, social relations, and agricultural productivity. I need not labour the point: whether or not the medieval Christian Church had the 'true' religion, people believed that it had and acted accordingly.

However, and this is the vital point, social constructions are viable only to the extent that they are *shared*. Fabrications they may be, but, if everyone believes them, then they are no longer beliefs; they are just 'how things are'. But a world-view that is shared by few people does not attain that solidity: it remains belief. If it is shared by very few or only one, it will be seen as madness.

So far I have simplified by supposing that what matters for the solidity of inter-subjectivity is numbers: the views of the many are accurate descriptions while the views of the few are pathologies to be rejected or remedied. This is important, because a world-view gains enormous plausibility from the unremarked repetition of mundane acts that embody it. When the response to every misfortune is prayer, when every parting is solemnized by saying 'God be with you' (the original of our *Goodbye*), when good weather is greeted with 'The Lord be praised', then the idea that the world was created by God is simply taken for granted. In this way, consensus gives great power to beliefs. But it is worth pointing out that not all views are equally powerful or persuasive: individuals and social groups differ in their ability to 'define the situation'. As Peter Berger put it: he who has the biggest stick has the best chance of imposing his views. We might add that what counts as a stick varies from society to society.

If how we see things and how we act is not 'natural' in the sense of flowing from our biology, but is only a product of our culture, does it follow that the socially constructed worlds that we inhabit are fragile and easily altered? The previous paragraph gives one answer in the negative. The chances of a child in Sicily in 1800 growing up to be anything other than a Catholic were remote. But most societies are not content to leave the plausibility of their culture to the weight of consensus. To use the term popularized by Marx, they also *reify* (from the Latin *re*, a thing, meaning 'to make thing-like').

If Gehlen and Durkheim are right that culture does for humans what instinctual and environmental constraints do for other species, then we must often choose to remain blind to its human origins. If we openly acknowledged the socially created nature of our arrangements and are

Sociology

too familiar with the fact that other peoples do things differently, our institutions would lose conviction.

In practice we have a wide variety of devices for reification. To give an example from the purely personal level, an elderly female acquaintance of mine does not 'drink coffee'. Instead, at the same time every day, she has 'coffee time': a formulation that implies that she is adhering to a timetable not of her own devising. Her coffee breaks are presented as an obligation. 'Coffee time' requires not only coffee but a biscuit, because 'a drink is too wet without one'. As someone who has spent very little of her long life in paid employment, her schedules are very obviously her own choices, yet she sees her life as a series of obligations and even, just sometimes, derives pleasure from rebelling against them.

On a grander scale, we can observe that most societies seek extra legitimation for their institutions. Primitive hunters supposed that they hunted in this particular way because that was how the Pig Gods taught them to hunt. Medieval monarchs claimed divine support for kingship. The Victorian hymn writer who composed 'All Things Bright and Beautiful', with its lines 'The rich man in his castle, the poor man at his gate, God made them highly and lowly, and ordered their estate', had the specific intention of persuading the poor to accept their situation, and there is no doubt that the repeated singing of that popular hymn did something to discourage the lower orders from getting uppity. Just as societies differ in their sources of power, so they also vary in what can be claimed as additional legitimation for particular social arrangements. As in the three examples just given, religious societies ascribe authorship to God or gods. In nineteenth- and early twentieth-century Western Europe, when religious explanations became less persuasive, people started to claim scientific justifications for particular orders. So it was no longer God who had ordained the estates of the rich man and the poor man but their genetic material or, as economic conservatives such as Margaret Thatcher and Ronald Reagan would have had it, the mysterious but invincible rules of political economy. That societies differ in just who or what is thought to have created the social order concerns me less than this abstract point: the near universality of reification suggests that it serves a purpose greater than merely bolstering the powerful.

One reason reification is so common is that it contains a basic truth. None of us personally created the social institutions that shape our lives; we were born into them. The roles that structure our behaviour and encapsulate the expectations that others will have of us preceded our arrival and will endure (no doubt slightly modified) after we depart. Reality may be socially constructed, but, taken in its totality, it is not the work of any nameable individual and it certainly has little or nothing to do with any one of us. Language is a good example of the coercive nature of conventions. Of course it is devised by people, but its basic shape is presented to us. Though we may modify it (and one or two of us may actually author a significant change), our general sense is that we simply adopt what is already there.

To summarize, we can recognize that reality is socially constructed without supposing the reverse: that if we stop defining a situation as true then it will melt away. Social institutions can have enormous power, and simply 'de-constructing' them by showing their human origins (especially by showing that some groups benefit more than others from particular institutions) will not make them vanish.

Layers of construction: Men at work

Religious organizations have a habit of claiming that their structure is divinely ordained, but the human origins of government agencies, commercial corporations, factories, and other 'formal organizations' are readily admitted. Often we can name the people who created a particular organization or radically altered its structure. Yet even in this field sociology can be radical in 'exposing' discrepancies between what the formal structure is supposed to look like and how it actually works.

We can take the notion of social construction as an invitation to appreciate the difference between the original architect's drawings for a building and what was actually built.

An excellent example of this sort of study is Melville Dalton's 1959 *Men Who Manage*. To appreciate the importance of Dalton's work we should step back to Max Weber's writings on bureaucracy. Each member of the founding trinity of sociology had a big idea about how modern societies differed from their predecessors. For Marx, it was class. For Durkheim, it was the breakdown of shared norms. For Weber, it was the rise of rationality. I should here add a qualification that applies to all the contrasts given in this book. Though it simplifies our stories if we pretend it does, social development does not fall into neatly demarcated periods. There are very few clean breaks. Attitudes and habits common in one period give way to others only gradually, and many will survive in particular geographical regions and social groups. When sociologists talk about social change in terms of epochs, they are, like caricaturists, identifying and amplifying the most significant features of a society. If space permitted, everything said here would be accompanied by many qualifying details and exceptions. But it does not, so I will press on with the sweeping generalizations.

In a small group of people linked by social ties that endure over long periods of time and over many areas of business (which is what we imply with the term 'community'), interaction can be monitored and coordinated face to face. Someone who is a problem can be 'spoken to', shunned, and, if necessary, ostracized. Decisions can be arrived at by negotiation and consensus. As the small community is replaced by the large-scale society, both the numbers of people involved and the complexity of the matter in hand require a very different form of management. Twenty crofters who share common grazing can meet regularly to decide how many beasts each can graze on the common. The allocation of blocks of the North Sea for oil exploration and extraction requires formal organization.

One feature of modernization is the massive increase in rational bureaucracy. Bureaucracy is not an invention of industrial societies; as Weber notes, the ancient and medieval Chinese were rather good at it, and for most of twenty centuries the Christian Church has been bureaucratically organized. But Weber believes that modern societies differ from traditional ones in the extent to which life is dominated by rationality.

More will be said about this in Chapter 4; here I want to summarize Weber's account of modern organization. First, the modern bureaucracy distinguishes between the office and the individual who occupies it. When the Sheriff resigns, the power passes to the next holder of the office. The distinction between office and occupant also applies to rewards. The assets of an engineering company belong to the company and not to the official who happens to be managing director. As an incentive to take seriously the fate of the enterprise we may offer officials some shares in the company, but generally they are paid a salary that is independent of the company's assets. To see how things could be arranged differently, we could consider the medieval institution of tax farming. People bid for the position of tax collector by offering to raise for the king a certain amount in tax. They could then collect as much as they liked over and above what they had offered to deliver. This may have been efficient in delivering resources to the king but it encouraged tax collectors to bleed taxpayers. Our tax revenues are quite separate from the salaried income of the tax collector.

Secondly, the bureaucracy handles its affairs after the fashion of the division of labour in manufacturing. Complicated business such as fighting a war is broken down into component parts so that for every job there is one and only one responsible office. The armaments section organizes the production of weapons; the medical corps treats the wounded; the pay office arranges for soldiers to be paid; and so on. As well as ensuring that everything that needs to be done is done and is done only once, such a division of labour allows officials to become expert in their specialized business. It also means that new officials can be trained and tested in the specific skills needed for the job, and expertise can provide a sensible yardstick for determining promotion.

Within task sections, offices are arranged in a clear hierarchy with unambiguous chains of command. All officials know to whom they answer and who answers to them.

Finally the work of officials is shaped by rules that are applied universally. All cases (for they are 'cases' rather than people) are dealt with in the same way and are judged only on the matter in hand. Modern tax collectors do not charge their friends, relatives, and co-religionists less than they charge strangers; they apply the same rules to all taxpayers.

At first sight and at a distance, this model offers an entirely convincing account of a major difference between modern and traditional societies. The German Army in 1900, the Church of England after its nineteenth-century reforms, or the US Internal Revenue Service provide ample illustrations. However, Weber's depiction also reads like a public-relations exercise. Indeed many of the self-descriptions offered by government agencies and private companies in the first part of the twentieth century read as if they had been written by someone thoroughly familiar with Weber's account of rational bureaucracy.

Dalton's scepticism about the rationality of modern organizations stemmed from his own experiences in the early 1950s working as a junior manager in two manufacturing firms in a US city he calls Magnesia. While doing his day job, he observed the way in which he and his colleagues actually worked. He concluded that there was a considerable gulf between the formal structures and operating procedures and how the companies actually operated. The prevailing ideology of management in those days was that it was 'scientific', following essentially rational methods to the single best solution for a problem. Dalton shows management to be a self-interested political activity, involving negotiation, compromise, and the recognition that there is no single solution. Dalton penetrates the idealized model of human behaviour presented by business schools and corporations as the way managers behave and shows the reality: they do things because they work and then call on the rules of the organization to give a semblance of rationality to decisions that were made on highly pragmatic and practical grounds.

I will give just three of his many illustrations. One company had very tight controls over spare parts and materials, which could be signed out of the store only on the production of a docket that identified the job for which they were required. However, the production line managers believed that keeping stocks of spare parts and materials on hand prevented costly delays. To discourage such hoarding, the company required unannounced audits of stock by certain management personnel. But the people who checked on the production managers also needed to work with them. So, instead of making unannounced inspections, the checkers made sure that word got around when a stock inspection was going to take place and which routes they were going to follow around the factory. The production managers kept their illicit supplies on trolleys so that they could shift them rapidly out of the inspection route. Thus the checkers met the company's formal requirements while maintaining good relationships with the production staff and letting them get on with their jobs.

Dalton was also interested in appointments and promotions. He discovered that a disproportionate number of senior managers were members of the Masonic Lodge and also members of the Yacht Club. They had apparently been appointed because they were 'one of us'. They were able to manipulate the informal machinery of political bargaining and strategic exchange in order to get things done. They were also members of informal cliques that commanded respect. Although these characteristics were not part of the formal criteria for management selection, Dalton is able to show how, from the point of view of the management, they made practical sense.

A third example of the gulf between rhetoric and reality concerns the hierarchy of authority and the power of offices. The companies for which Dalton worked followed Weber's model of having a clear structure of who answered to whom and clear demarcation of remit. However, of managers who formally shared the same status, some were much more powerful and influential than others. Lower officials had a very clear sense that certain of their superiors were of little account and could have their jobs dealt with last, while others were 'coming men' who should be given undue respect. In part this reflected competence; not all holders of formally equal offices were equally good at their jobs. In part it was a reflection of commitment. One man was fairly close to retirement and wanted nothing more than a quiet life, whereas another was young and ambitious and took every opportunity to increase the power of his office. In the language of roles we could say that, as for Shakespeare's *Hamlet*, the parts were scripted but the actors retained considerable freedom in the way they acted out the role.

That the reality of a complex organization did not mirror its formal structure is no longer a surprise. I would not like to fix a starting date to the spread of cynicism and the popularity of the exposé, but cultural products such as Siegfried Sassoon's diaries of life in the trenches in the First World War or Spike Milligan's tales of life in the British army in the Second have been available for most of the twentieth century. We are now well used to the point Dalton makes, but that it is now a truism does not stop it being true and important. Apparently well-defined formal organizations are constantly shaped and reshaped by the activities of those who inhabit them. This is not to say that they are chaotic and disorganized. It just means that the original theorists of formal organizations mislocated the *site* of formality. Dalton's companies functioned well because they were defined by reasonably clear goals (though these were sometimes in conflict) that were well understood by the managers and workers. They created and maintained their own practical understandings of how to go about the business and they also learnt how, if called upon to account for themselves, to present their actions *as if* they followed logically from the formal structures and operating procedures.

Layers of construction: Rule-breakers

That reality is repeatedly reconstructed in layers can be illustrated with the example of law and law-breakers. There is no doubt that law is a human product. Books of political science and jurisprudence can name the people who make it. In the United Kingdom, Parliament makes the law. In the United States, Congress and the Senate make federal law while the legislatures of the states make state law. In addition we can note that, although judges and justices are supposed only to interpret and apply, their applications can themselves create new law. In some cultures – Iran under the Mullahs, for example – supernatural legitimation is sought for the law by claiming that it is divinely ordained but even here we can identify the Mullahs whose interpretation of the Koran has shaped the *Shari'a* or religious law.

We can take the existence of the law as our starting point and suppose that we can readily read off what will count as law-breaking. We identify a particular act – man forces his sexual attention on reluctant woman – and, by holding it up to the template of the law, see if it is criminal or not. Unfortunately, it is not so simple. In the first place many laws are in themselves ambiguous. Even very detailed laws cannot specify how they are to be applied in every conceivable case. Secondly, many acts are potentially governed by many laws and the fit between them is not always neat. Laws accumulate. Framers may do their best to harmonize new and existing legislation, but there will inevitably be clashes, so that, even when the act in question is not contested, what body of law should be used to judge it may well be.

Furthermore, laws are rarely applied consistently. Take the relatively simple matter of driving faster than the speed limit. On British trunk roads, the speed limit is 60 miles an hour. However, traffic police very rarely stop people for doing 65 because measuring equipment and car speedometers are not accurate enough to be sure of intent to disregard the limit. But even this new 'real' limit is not applied evenly. My local police force has more calls on its time than it can meet and speeding on country roads is low priority. When there is nothing much else on, a traffic team will park behind a row of beech trees on a straight section where motorists habitually exceed the limit and they nab a few motorists. They will then go back to more pressing matters. Thus the chances of being caught speeding depend on the press of other calls on police time. Furthermore, how the police respond to a speeding driver will depend not only on the 'facts' of the matter (such as speed and road conditions), but also on such intangibles as the attitude and demeanour of the driver. If the motorist appears to be the sort of person who does not habitually disregard speed limits, then a stern word is the most likely sanction. If the driver is aggressive and 'seems like a speeder', then a booking and fine are more likely. In deciding how to respond, the police ask not only 'Has an offence been committed?' but also 'Is this person likely to offend again?'.

So we begin with the simple formula that crime is that which breaks the law and quickly discover that the matter is considerably more complicated. Indeed there seem to be so many filtering layers of decision-making and interpretation that we would be more accurate to say (a) that *crime is that which the appropriate officials have decided breaks the law* and (b) that the grounds for such decisions include many considerations that are 'extra-legal' or (as in the example of the police guessing about the future behaviour of the putative criminal) have at best a complex social relationship to matters of law. This would already be a significant elaboration on our starting point, but, of course, the police are not the only people who have a part in identifying criminals. The prosecuting authority has to decide whether to prosecute or not, and, if so, for what offence. Judges and juries have to try the case and arrive at a verdict.

The criminal justice system is a complex process of repeated social constructions, with each element driven by its own interests and with each element influenced by decision-making at other stages. The police handling of domestic violence offers a good example of such feedback. In the 1960s it was common for the police to ignore 'domestics'. They justified this by noting that the victims of domestic violence often refused to give evidence in court and that courts often failed to convict or, if they did convict, handed down slight punishments. For police forces with more than enough business to consume their resources, 'domestics' did not seem worth the trouble. However, this began to change in the 1970s when organized women's groups managed to draw media attention to violence in the home. This, in turn, influenced judges, who became less tolerant of it. New arrangements were devised to reduce the stress on complainants (at the investigation and prosecution stages), which in turn led to more complaints being made, to witnesses being more willing to give evidence, and to the police calculation of 'reward for effort' changing in favour of more robust action. So we gradually see the social constructions of domestic violence changing.

The idea that there is a large body of family crimes of violence, of which a shifting proportion gets reported, recorded, processed, and tried, still assumes that the raw material of the justice process is a world of actions that unambiguously divide into crimes and non-crimes. However, a more radical view is possible. If it is the case that the 'actual' status of the original act has less bearing on the final outcome than the various considerations that intervene at the filtering stages, then is it not more accurate to say that the acts of social definition or *labelling* are actually the source of criminality? A moral philosopher or a policeman may want to say that 'crime-ness' is a property of the original acts and that some crimes are discovered while others go undetected. If we are interested in the consequences of actions in the real world, it might be better to see 'crime-ness' as a property of the labels that official definers attach to certain acts.

The 'labelling' perspective on crime and deviance, which became popular in the late 1960s and obviously owed much of its appeal to its apparently radical attitude to social order, is most convincing when applied to ambiguous and borderline cases. A rugby club dinner results in considerable damage to a hotel; is this high jinks or serious hooliganism? An elderly lady believes that aliens have taken over her TV set; is this eccentricity or mental illness? A small shopkeeper massages his tax returns; is this fraud or entrepreneurial imagination? The body of a fisherman is found tangled in his rigging; is this suicide or accidental death? Given that there is obviously a lot of room for arriving at quite different interpretations of these acts or events, the labelling approach seems justified. It has the great advantage of drawing our attention to the fact that the final labels will owe as much to creative interpretation as to discovery. And it allows us to see the wide variety of interests that are involved in such interpretations. We can hazard the following guesses. Criminal damage done by the upper-class rugby club will be defined as 'high spirits', whereas the same acts committed by working-class football fans will be regarded as vandalism. If the elderly lady is financially self-sufficient and is not an essential figure in a family unit, then her oddities are more likely to be tolerated than to become the focus for treatment. The businessman who cheats to preserve 'his own money' from the taxman will be less severely punished than a social-security fraud who steals 'other people's money', even if each is similarly damaging the common good. If the deceased fisherman has relatives and belongs to a conservative religious tradition, his ambiguous death is more likely to be judged an accident than if he is single and secular. In all these examples we can see that whether a particular act is judged to be a crime or to be deviant is not explained by any quality of the act itself but by other considerations that enter into the process of labelling or definition.

However, important though this is in giving us a more realistic account of crime and deviance, the labelling approach exaggerates by neglecting two important points about social definitions. The first is that some social rules are actually quite simple. In any particular society or subculture there may be such consensus that we can often leave aside the process of social definition identified as central in the labelling approach. While some brutal physical contacts can be explained away ('she fell down the stairs') and others justified ('I though he had a knife and was going to stab me'), there remains a huge range of cases that very few of us would have difficulty *correctly* labelling as 'assault with a deadly weapon', 'grievous bodily harm', 'murder', and the like. While a wide range of strange behaviour can be tolerated as eccentricity, a similarly wide range would with little hesitation be taken as symptoms of madness requiring therapy. That is, although we know that something is a crime or is deviant only because it is defined as such by society (the labelling point), such definitions may become so well established that they are fairly evenly applied by most people.

The second weakness of labelling is that it rather overlooks conscience. This allows me to introduce formally the idea of *internalization*. Taken at its most robust, the labelling approach means that the crime that goes undefined is not a crime. Yet ten years after he had killed his wife and buried her under the patio, a man walked into a police station, asked to talk to a detective, and confessed. He did so because he had been tormented by guilt. He did not need any external authority to label his act a crime; his own conscience had already done that. Although his socialization into the norms of his culture had not been so complete as to prevent him killing, he had sufficiently internalized those rules that the voice of society within him had prevented him from being at ease with what he had done.

Talking of conscience allows me to restate a point implicit in the first section of this chapter: humans become social when the external contours of their culture are replicated inside their minds and their personalities. To return to the theatrical metaphor used earlier, in a stable successful society the actors do not just read through their parts. They are 'method actors' who have been so thoroughly steeped in their parts that they do not act them, they live them. The external aids of scripts and stage directions are no longer necessary. The actors have taken on the characters.

A large part of sociology is concerned with trying to understand how that happens. One of the key principles of sociology is that how people see themselves is greatly affected by how others see them. I have already identified one large-scale version of this phenomenon when I talked about society as a system of interlocking roles. To be a father requires that there be sons and daughters. To be a teacher requires that there be students and pupils. To be a good father requires that sons and daughters think of you as a good father and that others (spouse, grandparents of your offspring, friends, and neighbours) share this view.

This can be put in personal dynamic terms when we appreciate the part that the responses of others play in *learning* a role. A man tentatively acts in ways he thinks appropriate to a good father. He then reflexively monitors the responses of his children and of others close to him who observe those performances and modifies his actions in the light of how he thinks others see him. If he senses approval, he can take pride and pleasure in what he has done. When he sees hostility, lack of understanding, fear, and loathing, he may feel ashamed. The great American social psychologist Charles Horton Cooley coined the phrase 'the looking-glass self' to describe this process of acquiring an identity by responding to what we see of ourselves in the eyes of others. Sometimes such monitoring is formal and overt: the man and his wife may argue about the principles of good parenting. More often the monitoring is so low key as to be almost unconscious.

An important consequence for identity of social interaction is that attempts to identify who or what someone is can become *self-fulfilling*. If a young girl repeatedly fails to tidy her room, be ready on time, and collect the appropriate equipment for even simple tasks, her father may repeatedly depict her as an 'airhead': cute but incompetent. If this sort of designation and its implied explanation is repeated sufficiently often, by both parents and other close relatives and friends, the girl may well come to internalize that image of herself. She learns to think of herself as incompetent and comes more and more to act the part. What was intended as a valid act of describing an existing character actually creates what it thought it had observed.

A number of important qualifications need to be added to this account. First, the person being labelled is not passive. Identity is *negotiated*. The girl may find ways of responding to her father's view of her other than simply conforming to it. Her father, in turn, may find new ways of understanding her behaviour that, for example, turn 'airhead' into 'spiritually aware child'. Furthermore, not all of those who interact with the girl will be equally influential. George Herbert Mead talked of 'significant others'. For the child, parents (or their surrogates) will be the most significant others, but older friends and other relatives can also be influential. In later life people who occupy formal positions become significant and we may even be influenced by the supposed views of abstract 'reference groups'. In writing this book, I am aware of the likely responses of the community of sociologists.

A large body of research in the sociology of education very effectively uses the self-fulfilling prophecy to explain how schools inadvertently reproduce social class. We know from repeated surveys that children of working-class parents have a much higher chance of themselves ending up in manual work than the children of middle-class parents. We also know that this remains the case even when we compare children with the same IQ levels. Yet we also know that few teachers consciously discriminate against lower-class children or deliberately give them undeservedly poor marks. So how is class reproduced? The answer is, of course, complex. Housing patterns tend to reflect social class, so that neighbourhood schools in turn vary in class composition. Schools in middle-class areas tend to attract better teachers and gain reputations for good discipline and good exam results, which in turn attracts more middle-class parents and ambitious and self-confident working-class parents. Middle-class schools also tend to be better funded. But, even recognizing those large background considerations, it remains the case that, within any school, the performance of the children tends to be heavily influenced by class.

The explanation lies in a vicious circle. Working-class children begin with low expectations. They generally aspire only to the sorts of jobs done by their parents and close relatives. These same role models inhabit a 'rough' culture that leads their children to be louder and rougher than middle-class children. They tend to be more disruptive and difficult even when they have no particular intention of being so. They work less well and (and this is the crucial point), even when they work as well as other children, their virtues tend to be overlooked because teachers quickly form an estimation of how well certain children will do, and those expectations are based on subtle cues that have strong class components. In many often unconscious ways, those expectations are fed back to the children, so that they have a sense of 'failing' even before they come to formal tests of achievement. The expectations are further reinforced in those school systems where children are 'streamed' by ability.

Once children start patently to fail, they have a choice. Either they can continue to conform to the official value system of the school and see themselves as 'failures', or they can seek other sources of self-esteem. The latter is an option because older children who have already experienced failure have created an oppositional subculture of kids who pride themselves on acts of rebellion and who enjoy 'taking the piss out of the teacher'. I can recall one boy at my school (in the days when corporal punishment was commonplace) who fell foul of the staff early on in his school career and who thereafter prided himself on being so hard that no one could break him. In his confrontations with staff he deliberately upped the ante in order to prove that no one could belt him often enough or hard enough to make him cry. Not surprisingly, staff quickly came to view him as a problem to be managed and he left school at the earliest opportunity with no formal qualifications.

What we have here is a situational theory of learning. It supposes that those who feel devalued because they are judged to be failing in one particular system of values may be drawn to a counter-culture, one which reverses the dominant values. In order to feel good about themselves, the bad boys create their own subculture in which 'bad' is really good.

The above draws on the social psychology of Mead and Cooley to argue that consistently treating people as if they were a certain sort of person may make them just that. However, we can tell a slightly different version of the same sort of story in which the actor's acceptance of the judgements of others is less important. Let us suppose a middle-management accountant is wrongly accused of fraud. Despite protesting his innocence, he is convicted and imprisoned. He loses his job. His wife leaves him and takes the children. He loses his house and his financial security. On release from prison he finds that he can no longer work as a straight accountant. He is ostracized by former friends and associates, expelled from the golf club, and shunned by his local church. The exclusion from straight society is in pointed contrast to the acceptance he finds from criminals. In jail he mixed with people who did not despise him because of his supposed crimes. Though he continues to deny his guilt he finds that there is a society of people who admire him for what he is supposed to have done.

In those circumstances our accountant may well find himself open to offers from criminals. Instead of dissuading him from further crime, the fact of having been labelled a criminal may be sufficient to make him what, if we believe his protestations of innocence, he was not. In summary, certain kinds of labelling can have very similar consequences whether or not the original label was earned because those who do the defining have the power to impose their definitions.

The labelling approach is not just an abstract posture; it underpins our juvenile justice system. Although societies differ in what age they use as the cut-off, most modern states attempt to handle the crimes of young people in such a way as to minimize the chances of them being pushed out of conventional roles and into criminal careers. So our courts attempt to protect the identities of young offenders and, if they must be incarcerated, segregate them from adult prisoners who could provide role models.

I would now like to return to the general theme of this section. What the above discussions of crime and deviance, and of educational failure, show is that the creative element in social action is not confined to the birth of some institution. It is quite possible for orthodox Christians to be physicists. They can acknowledge that God made the earth but set that aside as they continue to study the regularities of the behaviour of matter. They simply suppose that, having made the laws of physics, God takes no further hand in their day-to-day operation. The relationship between people and the social reality they construct is quite different. We cannot acknowledge that our culture is a social product and then suppose that we can study social life without repeated reference to the creative interpretation that such a proposition implies. Instead we have to appreciate that social order is constantly fluid, ever in flux. While there is much value in understanding societies as collections of interlinked roles, guided by bodies of rules, we must always remember that the performance of some roles offers considerable scope for improvisation and the process of interpretation never stops.

Chapter 3
Causes and Consequences

Hidden causes

In the previous chapter I made the obvious point that, while reality is socially constructed, it none the less has an enduring and oppressive quality because the part that any one of us plays in that construction is trivial. Even our conscious rebellions against order, our 'escape attempts', tend to follow preordained lines. One of the ways that sociology differs from common sense is in challenging our fond image of ourselves as authors of our own thoughts and actions. It is not that we often think of ourselves as masters of our own destiny. Captains of industry, religious visionaries, and political leaders may see themselves as free spirits, but most of us have a pretty good idea of where we are on the totem pole. None the less, our very sense of identity presupposes that there is an 'I' independent of the ebb and flow of social forces. I may not be able to prevent my standard of living being affected by changes in the interest rate, but I can decide what food I eat, which political party I will support, which church (if any) I will attend, and how I will decorate my dwelling.

Yet, if there is to be any explanation of human behaviour, there must be regular patterns to life, and those regularities will at least partly be caused by forces outside our control and our cognition. The paradox between freedom and constraint was neatly expressed by Karl Marx when he said that we make our own fate but not in the circumstances of our own choosing. The 'making our fate' bit is easy to see, as are the more immediate constraints. I decide where to drive on a Sunday afternoon and I am aware that the way I drive is shaped by traffic regulations. But much of who we are and what we do has social causes that are obscure to us. By searching for regular patterns and by systematic comparisons between worlds, the sociologist can illuminate those causes.

A good example of research that finds social causes of what we take to be highly personal behaviour is the link between love and social identity. In many societies marriages are arranged by parents who select partners for their children with an eye to the value of alliances between families. With some exceptions (the residual aristocracy, for example) people in industrial societies pride themselves on being free from such extraneous considerations and suppose they select purely on the nebulous but strongly felt emotional grounds of love. Those who continue to use the older form can serve as jokes. *Blind Date* is a popular television show in which an eligible young man or woman selects a date from three contestants of the other gender who can be seen by the audience but not by the person choosing. The only information the selector gets is a few jokey answers to jokey questions. The resulting date is filmed and the pair are invited back to a subsequent show to talk about each other. In Britain in 1997 a number of Jewish businessmen floated the idea of founding a Jewish television channel. When asked about programme content, one of them joked that the channel might feature a version of *Blind Date* in which the contestant's mother gets to pick the date.

To the modern Western mind, it would seem a betrayal of true emotion to chose a spouse on the criteria of wealth, education, or occupational background. Yet when one dispassionately compares such demographic and socio-economic characteristics of spouses one finds that the choices apparently made on the grounds of love and affection none the less show very clear social patterns. While rarely conscious of compromising love with extra-emotional considerations, most people marry others of the same religion, race, class, and educational background. Our social groups effectively socialize us to see particular dress and hair styles, modes of demeanour and address, accents and vocabularies as being more attractive than others. Although the choice seems personal, what draws us to a certain person (or repulses us about another) is much the same as what a diligent matchmaker would bear in mind when choosing a mate for us.

The same point can be made about many of our beliefs and attitudes. We may believe that we hold our views because we have dispassionately examined the evidence and come to the correct appreciation, but social surveys show repeatedly that much of what we believe can be predicted from such social characteristics as gender, race, class, and education. One might have thought that being religious was a highly personal matter, but in every industrial society (and in many others) women are clearly more devout and pious than men, however one measures those properties.

Of course, not everyone always wishes to claim ownership of his or her actions. No modern discussion of the extent to which we are shaped by social forces would be complete without some mention of the cult of the victim. In any society there will be times when people wish to deny responsibility for their actions. Religious people blame divine displeasure or satanic influence. In secular cultures, society itself can be blamed for those of our actions that we would disavow. As Terry put it in the *Minder* joke mentioned in the Preface, his friend is still thieving but now that he has a degree in sociology he knows why he does it. If Durkheim is right that the suicide rate for a society is determined by the twin social properties of 'regulation' and 'integration', then the responsibility of any individual for his or her suicide must be limited. Even more so in Marx's model of social evolution through class conflict. If we are what we are because of our relationship to the means of production (our 'class') and if we are borne along by the dynamics of class conflict, then we can hardly be held accountable for our fate. The interactionist sociology of Mead and Cooley, seen in its most radical form in the labelling theory of crime, similarly frees us from our own actions. If we become what others accuse us of being, then it is their fault.

Such popularized versions of sociological explanations are the lifeblood of those television talk shows in which sad people blame everyone else but themselves for their petty tragedies. If you are incapable of maintaining satisfactory personal relationships, well, that is because your father abused you as a child. Even if you do not recall being abused, the novel theory of 'rediscovered memories' allows you to claim that he actually did, although you did not know it until an abuse therapist helped you to introspect in middle age. Drug addicts, alcoholics, bulimics, anorexics, and sex addicts line up to claim social causes of their problems. There is perhaps no surprise in this. I will say more later about the relationship between the individual and the social roles he or she plays, but the fact that we can see the two things as separate allows us to be self-interestedly selective about what we wish to claim as the real 'me' and what we dismiss as the product of social conditioning.

Professional sociology differs from its lay counterpart here in a number of ways. First, it aims to be even-handed and disinterested. Ordinary people usually wish to blame society for their troubles but claim their successes for themselves. Sociologists are as interested in the social causes of health, wealth, and happiness as they are in illness, poverty, and depression. Secondly, it aims to be led by the evidence. Thirdly, it is concerned with the general and the typical rather than with the individual. Of course, the only way we can study the experiences of the typical unskilled industrial worker, for example, is by collecting information about hundreds of individual industrial workers, but it is the elements of their experiences that are common which concern us, not those parts that are unique. The amateur sociologist draws on supposedly general explanations to understand his or her life; the professional studies the individual lives in order to generalize.

Unintended consequences

One of the strands of the sociological bracelet is the ironic principle of unanticipated outcomes. As the Scottish poet Robert Burns succinctly put it: 'the best laid plans of mice and men gang aft aglay.' We set out to do one thing. Because we are unaware of all the social forces that shape us and because we cannot anticipate how our actions will be received by others, we end up achieving something very different. I will illustrate the point with two examples that concern the links between ideas and the organizations that people create to promote those ideas.

Robert Michels, a student of Weber who was active in left-wing politics in Germany in the first decade of the twentieth century, was struck by a common pattern of evolution in left-wing trade unions and political parties. They began as revolutionary or radical attempts to reconstruct the world but became increasingly conservative and at peace with the world. They began as primitive democracies but became less and less democratic. In what at first sight looks like a very different arena, the world of conservative Protestant sects, H. Richard Niebuhr identified a similar pattern. The Methodist movement in the late eighteenth century was radical. It broke away from the Church of England because it wished to return to a more pristine Christianity. Initially it preached the need to restructure the world but gradually became socially conservative. Initially it stressed the priesthood of all believers but gradually acquired a professional clergy.

That we see the same pattern being repeated suggests that it is not accidental and hence can be explained by reference to some general social processes. That the consequences were so different from those desired by any of the people involved suggests that we cannot explain what happened simply be saying that these people wished that outcome.

The explanation Michels proposed went as follows. Any kind of group activity requires organization. But as soon as one starts to organize one creates a division within the movement between the organized and the organizers, between ordinary members and officials. The latter quickly acquire knowledge and expertise that set them apart and give them power over ordinary members. The officials begin to derive personal satisfaction from their place in the organization and seek ways of consolidating it. They acquire an interest in the continued prosperity of the organization. For ordinary trade unionists, their union is just one interest in which they have a small stake. But for the paid officials the union is their employer. Preserving the organization becomes more important than helping it achieve its goals. As radical action may bring government repression, the apparatchiks moderate.

At the same time as material interests dispose them to compromise their once radical credentials, the officials are drawn into new perspectives by a new 'reference group'. They come to appreciate that they share more in common with the officials of other political parties than with their own rank and file. Like servants discussing their masters, Labour and Conservative party activists can swap stories about the idiocies of the people they represent and they can exchange 'recipes' for organizational efficiency.

Niebuhr's account of the decline of radicalism among Protestant sects is similar. The first generation of members deliberately and voluntarily accepted the demands of the sect. They made sacrifices for their beliefs. The people who broke away from the State churches in England and Scotland in the eighteenth and early nineteenth centuries sometimes suffered political, social, and financial penalties. The State could confiscate their property, exclude them from holding political office or military rank, and remove their children to have them raised as good

Anglicans. In so far as they made sacrifices for their beliefs, the founding generation of sectarians invested more than just their hopes in the new faith, and their commitment, thus tested, was all the greater. But subsequent generations, the children and grandchildren of the sect founders, did not join voluntarily. They were born into it, and, however much effort was put into socializing them into the sect's ideology, it was inevitable that their commitment would be less than that of their parents.

This was even more so the case if the sectarians, by working diligently to glorify God and avoiding expensive and wasteful luxuries, had achieved a status and standard of living considerably more comfortable than that of their own parents. The children of most first-generation Methodists were moving up in the world and hence had more to lose by remaining so much at odds with it. They mixed with others of more elevated status than their parents. They were a little embarrassed at the roughness and lack of sophistication of their place of worship, their uneducated minister, their rough folk hymns and liturgies. They began to press for small adaptations towards a more respectable format, more comparable to that of the established church.

There is a further point that mirrors exactly what Michels noted about political parties. Although most sects began as primitive democracies, with the equality of all believers and little or no formal organization, gradually a professional leadership cadre emerged. Especially after the founding charismatic leader had died, there was a need to educate and train the preachers and teachers who would sustain the movement. There was a need to coordinate the growing organization. There were assets to be safeguarded and books to be published and distributed. With organization came paid officials and such people had a vested interest in reducing the degree of conflict between the sect and the surrounding society. The clergy of other religious organizations came to displace the sect's lay members as the crucial reference group. The sect clergy came to feel they deserved the status and levels of education, training, and reward enjoyed by their professional peers.

Niebuhr saw the sect as a short-lived form of religious organization, gradually becoming more tolerant, lax, and more upwardly mobile, and eventually becoming a denomination. This pattern can readily be found. It often takes more than one generation, but the development of the Methodists in the fifty years after Wesley's death fits the picture, as do the changes among the Quakers in the late eighteenth and nineteenth centuries. The austere commitment of early followers, with their distinctive mode of plain dress (with wide-brimmed hats for the men, who conspicuously refused to doff them for the King) and distinctive forms of speech, gave way to more conventional styles. The early Quakers would not have read a novel or attended the theatre, but the 'Gay Quakers' (as they were known), usually the offspring of wealthy merchants, manufacturers, and bankers, became more and more like the Church of England neighbours with whom they mixed as social equals. By the middle of the nineteenth century one finds them crossing over into first the evangelical wing and then the mainstream of the Church of England.

The Niebuhr pattern captures an important truth but it needs certain qualifications. Niebuhr tends to concentrate on the pressures for change within the sect and rather underestimates the influence of changes in the external world of the sect. For example, in the periods under discussion the economy was growing rapidly and standards of living generally were rising. The temptations to compromise would be considerably fewer and weaker in a static or declining economy. Secondly, the rise of a professional clergy and a bureaucratic structure is often described as though it followed from moral weakness on the part of the sectarians when it is in large part thrust upon any group in the modern world by the expectations of the rest of the society. Professionalism and bureaucracy are just the means by which modern societies organize things, and many sectarians find themselves obliged by the need to negotiate various forms of recognition from the State (the right to be conscientious objectors, or to avoid property taxes, for example) to become more organized.

Further, Niebuhr exaggerates the extent to which Protestant sects are much of a muchness. As Bryan Wilson has argued in detail, doctrinal differences between sects make them variously susceptible to the sort of accommodation Niebuhr describes. We need not pursue the differences further than noting that sects can organize themselves and their relations with their surrounding society so as to remain sectarian for many generations. The drift towards the denominational compromise is a common career but it is not inevitable.

These examples neatly illustrate the reverse consequence of the human capacity for reflexive thought. People can call on sociological explanations to provide justifications for their behaviour, and to console themselves if they cannot or will not change. But people can learn from their past mistakes and they can learn from sociological accounts of their actions. Although Michels' conclusions are commonly titled 'the iron law of oligarchy' and Niebuhr's thesis is often treated as if it had similarly identified a basic law of social evolution, these are not laws in the natural-science sense. It may be rare but it is possible for anarchists to avoid the pull towards compromise and respectability. Radical political movements can remain true to their initial ethos, even when it results in their destruction. Sects can resist the pull to denominational respectability. The Seventh Day Adventists have blunted the threat from the increased prosperity of their members by ensuring that much of that prosperity and the subsequent improvements in living standards are channelled through the organization and thus tie in members more completely. Communitarian sects such as the Amish and the Hutterites have also found ways of avoiding the more obvious pitfalls. In the first place, they created prohibitions on the use of modern farming machinery and thus kept down their productivity. When, despite this, they became wealthy, they used the profits to buy new land and split their communities. This had the additional benefit of keeping communities to a size that allowed face-to-face communication and intimate personal contacts between all members. This in turn restrained the growth of formal structures of leadership and thus prevented Michels' oligarchy.

The point is that bromides always do what bromides do. People possess reflexive conscious and can think about what they do. This does not mean they can always master themselves or their circumstances, but it does mean that they can learn from their mistakes and from others. And they can learn from sociology. People who wish to start a commune can now read and learn from Kanter's studies. A class in my course on the sociology of religion was once stunned by a student who announced that she was taking the course because she planned to start her own religion and wanted some tips!

Chapter 4
The Modern World

The observer and the observed

Sociology has an unusual relationship with its subject matter. Although we can view it as a disinterested intellectual discipline that stands aside from the world it observes, sociology is itself a symptom of the very things it describes.

In his work on Puritans in science, Robert Merton argued that the religion of the Jews and then Christianity were rationalizing forces. By having just one God instead of a pantheon of deities (who often operated erratically and at cross purposes), and by confining God to creating and ending the world but not interfering much in between, Christianity permitted a scientific attitude to the material world because it assumed the world to be orderly. Furthermore, the material world was not itself sacred in any sense that inhibited its systematic study. Once the Reformation had rejected the authority of the Roman Church, scientists were free to pursue their scholarship unhindered by religious imperatives. According to Merton, what made modern science possible was not technical advances in instrumentation so much as a new way of looking at the world.

A similar case can be made for why sociology appears when it does. The fourteenth-century Arab philosopher Ibn Khaldun or the ancient Greeks Plato and Aristotle made sociological observations in the course of their philosophical and historical writings, but it is not until Adam Smith, David Hume, and Adam Ferguson at the end of the eighteenth century that we find, in what was collectively called the 'Scottish Enlightenment', a body of academic work that would be recognizable to modern sociologists, and it is not until the twentieth century that the discipline flourishes. This is not an accident. In a traditional society with a coherent and all-embracing culture, few but powerful social institutions, and an all-pervasive religion that adds divine authority to those social institutions, it is not easy to see the world as socially constructed. Though some people might know that things could be different and might even have travelled to foreign parts, the solidity of their own taken-for-granted social world would crush any relativizing impact of such knowledge. The weakening of traditions, the decline of religious legitimations for the social order, and increasing social diversity are all necessary preconditions for sociology.

Modernity

This seems a good point to spell out in a little more detail the distinctive features of modern times. By 'modernization' I mean the social consequences of an increase in the ratio of inanimate to animate power. Unless Von Daniken is right about the spacemen, the ancient Egyptian pyramids were built by men and beasts with only levers and inclined planes to lighten the burden. We build with machines driven by fossil fuels, which massively increases our productive capacity. This account of what follows from that can be no more than a cartoon sketch, but it will summarize what sociology sees as distinctive about the social formations that concern it (in contrast to the traditional societies that are studied by anthropologists).

Manufacturing work has become ever more finely divided. Tasks, and the people who perform them, have become so specialized that we are now hopelessly reliant on each other. The typical peasant of the Middle Ages owned nothing he could not make himself and the possessions of even the rich were produced by only a small number of tradesmen. Now even the poor of Japan or Germany will own goods made on the other side of the world and eat food shipped from another continent. Production has ceased to be a personal activity involving the family and the community. Exchange is conducted through the impersonal medium of cash (rather than barter) and is mediated by markets. Although people in industrial societies are far less self-reliant than their agricultural forebears, their helplessness does not strengthen personal bonds. It just increases the need for formal means of coordination. Instead of finding what we need through informal conversations on the village green, we use *Yellow Pages*.

The ever-finer division of labour in production is mirrored in the non-economic sphere as social institutions become increasingly specialized. Industrial societies are far more 'differentiated' than agrarian ones. A good example is the decline in scope of religious institutions. In the Middle Ages, the Christian Church provided not only access to supernatural power but also civil administration, education, poor relief, and social discipline. Now civil administration is the province of secular government departments, education is provided by nurseries, schools, and universities, welfare is provided by social-work agencies, and social control is managed by police forces, courts, and prisons.

Changes in the family provide further examples of increased specialization. In agrarian societies, the family was often a unit of production as well as the social institution through which we managed the biological and social reproduction of our society. In industrial economies, most economic activity is conducted in distinct settings; we leave home to go to work.

The rise of industrialization brought with it complex changes in the nature and social consequences of inequality. In theory people became more alike and in many ways the world became much fairer. At the same time the social distance between different sorts of people increased. Agrarian societies had considerable disparities of status, but most people lived similar lives and they lived cheek by jowl. In medieval tower houses and castles, the gentry and their servants often slept in the same room, separated only by curtains. The lord might have clean straw but lords and servants slept on straw. They ate at the same table, with the salt dish marking off the gentry from the riff-raff. Because the social structure was openly hierarchical, superiors did not feel threatened by the close proximity of their minions and could comfortably inhabit the same physical and mental space.

Industrialization destroyed the great pyramid of feudal social order. Innovation and economic expansion brought with them occupational mobility. People no longer did the job they had always done because their family had always done that job. Occupational change and social advancement made it hard for people to think of themselves as permanently inferior and as having a fixed 'station' in life. Furthermore, economic growth brought increased *physical* mobility and greater contact with strangers. Profound inequalities of status are only tolerable and harmonious if, as in the Hindu caste system, the ranking is widely known and accepted. Soldiers can move from one regiment to another and still know their place because there is a uniform (in both senses) ranking system. In a complex and mobile society, it is not easy to know whether we are superior or subordinate to this new person. Once people have trouble knowing who should salute first, they stop saluting. Basic equality becomes the norm.

The dynamic is reinforced by the separation of home and work. One cannot be a serf from sunrise to sunset and a free individual for the evening and at weekends. A real serf has to be full-time. A lead miner in Rosedale, Yorkshire, in 1800 might have been sorely oppressed at work, but in the late evening and on Sunday he could change his clothes and his persona to become a Methodist lay preacher. As such he was a man of high prestige and standing. The possibility of such alternation marks a crucial change. Once occupation became freed from an entire all-embracing hierarchy and became task specific, it was possible for people to occupy different positions in different hierarchies. That made it possible to distinguish between the role and the person who played it. Roles could still be ranked and accorded very different degrees of respect, power, or status, but it became possible to treat the people behind the roles as all being in some abstract sense equal. To put it the other way round, so long as people were seen in terms of just one identity in one hierarchy, then egalitarianism was difficult because treating alike a peasant and his feudal superior threatened to turn the entire world upside down. But once an occupational position could be judged apart from the person who occupied it, it became possible to maintain a necessary order in the factory, for example, while operating a different system of judgements outside the work context. The Ironmaster could rule his workforce but sit alongside his foreman as an elder in the local church. Of course, power and status are often transferable. Being a force in one sphere increases the chances of influence in another. The Ironmaster could expect to dominate the congregation, but he would only if his wealth was matched by manifest piety. If it was not, his fellow churchgoers could respond to any attempt on his part to impose his will by defecting to a neighbouring congregation.

In a nutshell, the fragmentation of the simple traditional society allowed the rise of autonomous individuals who were seen as being, at least in the abstract, much of a muchness.

The structural causes of egalitarianism reinforced, and were reinforced by, ideological pressures in the same direction. It is not coincidence that the first modern industrial societies were predominantly Protestant in religion. The sixteenth-century Reformation contained within it the seeds of the 'Liberty, Equality, Fraternity' that was preached by the French Revolution more than 200 years later. Martin Luther and John Calvin were not liberals in the modern sense. They held that all people were alike, but only in their sinfulness and before God. None the less, equality in the eyes of God laid the foundations for equality in the eyes of man and before the law. So long as society, polity, and economy were seen as a single unified and coherent universe, the inherent egalitarianism of the Reformation was compromised by the insistence of the powerful on maintaining the hierarchy, but, once that single universe had been broken into distinct sectors, the democratic potential could be realized.

The rise of democracy was hastened by one consequence of the Reformation that was coincidentally also a necessary condition for a modern economy and a modern nation state: the spread of literacy. A religion that says that salvation is acquired by obeying the priest class and following its rituals does not need its people to be docile and passive, but it does nothing to encourage the alternative. A religion that says that everyone must study the Word of God and take personal responsibility for obeying God's commands not only encourages personal autonomy but also needs to provide people with the ability to read the Word. So the first thing the Reformers did was to translate the Bible from Latin, the international language of the educated, into the many languages of the common people. The second thing they did was to teach people to read. The revolutionary potential of that was well understood. As late as the start of the nineteenth century Hannah More, an evangelical Christian who created a string of schools in the Mendips, tried to teach her pupils only to read, not to write. Writing was dangerously liberating, but reading, especially the series of socially conservative and morally uplifting tracts she produced, was safe. She failed in her mission. Her pupils took their new skills and turned them to their own needs.

The point about egalitarianism is often misunderstood. I am not suggesting that modernization swept away all differences of wealth and power. I am saying, with Karl Marx, that the class structure of industrial capitalism was simpler and more fluid than the hierarchies it superseded because it replaced the complex web of feudal obligations and reciprocal responsibilities with the simple contract. Where Marx was wrong was in his belief that classes would become ever more rigid as all other social divisions became replaced by what he called 'relationship to the means of production'. In Marx's vision there would be just two great classes: the capitalist, who owned the means of production, and the proletarians, who did not. Increasing conflict between these two blocs would eventually lead to the great and final revolution when private property would be swept away and communism would replace capitalism. Clearly Marx was wrong about the revolution, and that error stemmed from his mistake about the increasing rigidity of class divisions. Far from becoming ever more sclerotic, class divisions softened. As Weber pointed out, there were major divisions within Marx's classes. In Marxist theory, all proletarians were in the same (ever more leaky) boat, but, as Weber correctly saw, those who were alike in not owning productive capital could still be very different in power and hence in life chances. Those who possessed scare skills (professional workers, for example) could exert considerable command over their working conditions and enjoy considerable autonomy. There was also an important group of managers who, although they did not own capital, none the less, through their day-to-day control of capitalist enterprises, enjoyed a position quite different from that of unskilled workers. Furthermore, the rise of the joint stock company meant that an increasing amount of capital ceased to be owned by individuals and came instead to be owned by collective agents such as pension funds.

Marx also failed to appreciate the consequence of *flow* within occupational structures. Throughout the nineteenth and early twentieth centuries, the proportion of people who worked in agriculture steadily fell: farm labourers moved into the towns and cities and into the factories. In the twentieth century the proportion of people who work at unskilled manual production jobs has steadily fallen. In 1911 over three-quarters of Britain's employed population were manual workers. By 1964 this had fallen to half and by 1987 it was only a third. Even if we can view the class structure as a stable column of boxes (and more of that shortly), the content of those boxes has been in constant flux. People have moved in and out of them, often in only one generation, almost always in two. This offers one very powerful reason why people did not, as Marx expected, come to see themselves as being much defined by their class. They did not see themselves in those terms because they were not in any one social place long enough.

Weber's way of conceptualizing class in terms of 'market situation' or the amount of control people have over their working lives has proved much more fruitful than Marx's capital-and-labour schema. The now most commonly used method divides people as follows. Those in the service class or *salariat* exercise delegated authority or specialized knowledge and expertise on behalf of their employing organization. In return, they enjoy relatively high incomes, security of employment, incremental advances, enhanced pension rights, and a good deal of autonomy at work. The *working class* consists of skilled and unskilled manual workers who supply discrete amounts of labour in a relatively short term and specific exchange of effort for money. These occupations tend also to be more intensively supervised and controlled. Between the service class and the working class, we have the *routine clerical* class, which is defined by employment relations that combine elements of the service relationship and the pure labour contract. A fourth class consists of the *small proprietors and self-employed*, who enjoy the autonomy of the service class but also exchange effort for money on a 'piece' or time basis. Finally, we distinguish *farmers* and *agricultural workers*, whose working lives often differ markedly from those of other kinds of small proprietors and manual workers: they own land, involve their families in production, and offer and receive payment in kind (such as tied housing).

Although these divisions are more complex than what we commonsensically mean by class, this system has a number of advantages. First, the categories are based on a clear and testable theory about what matters for life chances. Secondly, they have repeatedly been shown to be effective in explaining social regularities. Thirdly, they have been extensively used in cross-national comparisons of social mobility.

By social mobility we mean the extent or ease of movement between classes and we usually have two questions in mind. How likely is it that someone will move from one class to another in his or her lifetime? How likely is it that people will end up in a class that is not the same as that of their parents? One of the most surprising results of modern class analysis is that the relative chances of changing position vary little from one society to another. We may suppose that such new or radically restructured societies as Japan, Australia, and the United States are much more open than Britain, but reliable studies have shown that these and ten other major industrial societies have very similar mobility regimes; that is, that they are similarly fluid. Furthermore, though those of us lucky enough to have benefited from the change in the class structure might find this hard to believe, relative class mobility chances have remained much the same throughout the twentieth century.

This finding surprises us because we commonly confuse the likelihood of any particular person 'getting on' with the *opportunity* for social advancement, which is largely determined by the structure of the system. I will explain. Whatever class you are born in, the odds of improving yourself depend not just on the fluidity of the system but also on the capacity of the box you want to end up in. Over the twentieth century the shape of the class hierarchy changed from a pyramid (small service class; large working class) to a lozenge, as the number of people involved in manual work declined and the white-collar and professional sectors grew rapidly. As a result of that change, everyone has had a better chance of moving up but the *relative* chances of someone from the bottom of the pile and someone from the top ending up at the top, have remained much the same. As Gordon Marshall puts it:

More 'room at the top' has not been accompanied by greater equality in the opportunities to get there. All that has happened is that proportionately more of the new salariat jobs have gone to the children of parents already holding privileged class locations. In sum the growth of skilled white-collar work has increased opportunities for mobility generally, but the distribution of those opportunities across the class has stayed the same.

In other words, children of the working class have benefited from the expansion of white-collar work, but then so have the children of the middle classes.

What we make of this will depend largely on what we want or expect. If we are interested in social justice, we might find it rather depressing that those at the top have retained their advantages. However, if what we are interested in is *absolute* social mobility, then we would still be impressed that so many working-class people have risen into the service class, even though there has not been a corresponding number of service-class people going the other way. That lots of people now have more comfortable and affluent lives owes far more to changes in the economy than to greater equality of opportunity, but that should not blind us to the scale of the change.

The expansion of the service class can serve as a link to the next element in my description of modernization: the rise of the nation state. We are so used to maps that divide the world into France, Germany, Italy, and the like, and to wars (real and metaphorical) between nations, that we can easily lose sight of the novelty of this way of dividing and organizing people. Ethnic groups, united among themselves and divided from their neighbours by religion and language, are ancient, but until the eighteenth century most economies and polities were both larger and smaller than the present nation: villages and towns for some things, monarchies (which might encompass a number of countries) and empires for others. The rise of the nation state brought with it the need for ever-increasing numbers of officials to staff its machinery of government. In the twentieth century the nation state became the welfare state and that created a vast array of professional middle-class jobs in health, social security, housing, and education.

That modern lives are organized more by nation states than by communities has paradoxical consequences for the links between society and culture. On the one hand, the nation state requires a certain degree of internal homogeneity and promotes a sense of shared identity through a common language and a national history (preferably a heroic one). It demands loyalty to the fatherland or motherland. But, at the same time, the modern nation state has to come to terms with considerable cultural diversity within its borders.

Diversity comes from various sources. People migrate and take their culture with them; this has been the experience of New World states such as the United States or Australia. The state may expand its territory to encompass new peoples, as happened with the expansion of Britain to become the United Kingdom. Unitary states may be created from a number of republics, kingdoms, and principalities, as with Germany and Italy. But modernization itself creates cultural diversity *within* a society. In the feudal world a single Church encompassed almost the entire population and imposed something like a unitary set of values and norms on the people. With industrialization, communities of like-situated people fragmented into classes that developed their own interests. This increased social diversity was reflected in the religious culture, which fragmented into competing organizations. The gentry (and the agricultural labourers they controlled) stayed with the national church; its hierarchical structure of archbishops, bishops, and priests suited well the aristocratic view of the world as a divinely ordained pyramid. But the urban merchants, skilled craftsmen, and the more independent farmers were drawn to more democratic forms of religion and supported a series of schisms. The details of the break-up of what was once a unified culture are less important than the consequence.

Faced with increasing social diversity, the State had a simple choice. It could try to coerce conformity or it could become tolerant. Usually toleration was the second preference, accepted only when the costs of coercion became too high to bear and accepted only recently. In Britain, it was not until the middle of the nineteenth century that the final restrictions on the civil liberties of religious dissenters were removed. Catholics in Scotland did not get the vote until 1829 (and in 1998 they were still barred from the throne). Oxford and Cambridge had religious tests for entry until the 1870s and it was not until 1891 that such tests for Members of Parliament were abolished. These were the last vestiges of attempts to preserve a national religious culture that had looked pretty shaky since the eighteenth century. Despite persecution, the Quakers became wealthy and powerful, and by the 1830s the Methodists and Baptists were too numerous to be excluded from public life. Increasing diversity, combined with the already described rise of egalitarianism, forced the State to become increasingly tolerant of cultural differences.

Long-term, cultural pluralism brought about fundamental changes in the structure of social life and in its psychology. At the societal level, we see an increasing division between the public and the private world. People became increasingly free to do what they liked at home, at leisure, in private. At the same time, toleration was increasingly enforced by procedural rules in the public sphere. Many illustrations of this momentous change can be seen in how we use the term 'discrimination'. In the early nineteenth century it was quite normal for someone who held a powerful public office to use it to promote the interests of his family and friends. Patronage was the key to social advancement. Large landowners who controlled church appointments, for example, were expected to give rich parishes or posts on the staff of cathedrals to their kinsmen or to the sons of other wealthy patrons who could return the favour. Senior army officers and civil servants would appoint their relatives. We would now regard such a system as unfair. Nepotism is no longer a descriptive term; it is an accusation. More than that (and this offers another important insight into the modern world) we would regard such a system as inefficient.

Modern societies take the principles that underlie the industrialization of manufacture and apply them to the organization of people in other spheres. We suppose that any task is best done if we concentrate on the matter in hand and relegate all other considerations. We thus expect that soldiers will be promoted because they show aptitude for the task of soldiering and not because they are the younger sons of generals. We expect that clergy will be appointed because they show appropriate spirituality and not because their families have some 'pull' with the patron of the parish. Admission to higher education is by academic qualifications. Concentration on the task in hand requires us to be 'universalistic'. For example, we suppose that the most efficient and fairest way of allocating government housing is to establish criteria of need (such as number of children and state of present housing) and then allocate houses as they become vacant to those who 'need' them most. When, as was the case in Birmingham in the early 1960s, we discover that local councillors are denying council houses to immigrants, we accuse them of 'discrimination' and we create new sets of rules and procedures to force housing allocation to be put on a rational basis.

Of course, powerful groups do not readily bow to the demands for civil rights and in many arenas we see lengthy cat-and-mouse games. When the United States gave the vote to blacks, many southern states tried to preserve white supremacy by creating requirements of voters (such as literacy tests) that superficially looked fair, in that they applied to everyone, but were actually intended to curb black voting. When, despite this, blacks began to vote in large numbers, electoral districts were drawn up in ways that reduced the effectiveness of the black vote. By creating a large number of low-density white congressional districts and a small number of districts that encompassed very large numbers of blacks, one white vote could be made as influential as three or four black votes. The response of the federal government and the courts was to promote new laws that prevented each new evading tactic.

The progress of civil rights in modern societies has been uneven and halting. For all our legislative efforts on equal opportunities, it remains the case that many groups are systematically disadvantaged. While we have a good record of promoting *individual* legal and political rights, and of trying to prevent discrimination, we have done less to redress the considerable disparities of power and wealth that flow from social characteristics such as class, gender, and race. Strategies for redistributing wealth or creating real equality of opportunity by giving disadvantaged groups various sorts of 'head start' have usually been defeated by the counter-argument that they infringe the individual rights of those who cannot claim membership of the group that is intended to benefit from 'affirmative action'. None the less, observing that our societies retain certain forms of inequality should not blind us to the extent to which they have abandoned others. Modern societies regard as unjust and inefficient, and seek strenuously to outlaw, discriminatory practices that were entirely acceptable 200 years ago.

To recap, on the one hand, we have the public sphere becoming increasingly free of cultural norms (such as 'promote your cousins'). On the other hand, we have ever-greater freedom for people to exercise their personal preferences. Religious preferences and sexual orientation are now largely matters for individuals. The important point the sociologist would make about these changes, which separates the sociological explanation from that of the idealist philosopher, is that increasing personal freedom and liberty did not come about because any particular person or group thought liberty was a good idea. It was not the sloganeering of the French revolutionaries or black civil-rights activists that made the world as it is. Such social movements merely reinforced changes that were already underway as a necessary accommodation to the forces of modernization. Changes in the economic and political structure required changes in our basic attitudes to people. The division of public from private was a necessary accommodation to increasing social and cultural diversity in a context that assumes all people are at base equal.

That describes the structural response to social fragmentation. There was also a powerful change in the way we hold our beliefs and values. We saw it first in religion, but it spread. When the dominant religious cultures first fragmented, each fraction insisted that it and only it was right, but with increased diversity such conviction became difficult to maintain. The easiest way to do it is to have a theory which both asserts the superiority of one's own views and explains why other peoples have got it wrong. The British missionaries of the nineteenth century developed the notion that God revealed himself in forms appropriate to the social evolution of different races. To the aborigines and Africans he gave animism. To the more developed Arabs he gave Islam. To the southern Europeans he gave Catholicism. But to the northern Europeans (and especially the British) he revealed himself fully by giving them evangelical Protestantism. We can appreciate the rich functionality of this line of thought. It explained why other people were wrong without accusing them of malevolence. It asserted the primacy of British Protestantism. And it justified the civilizing mission of British imperialism. By 'bringing on' these supposedly backward races we would raise them to the point where they were ready for the true religion.

This is one example of the devices that people can use to sustain their own views in the face of alternatives. Another is to suppose that those who disagree with us are in thrall to some evil power. So American fundamentalists of the cold-war era supposed that liberal Christians were either in the pay or the power of Soviet Communism. All of these strategies work best when the dissenters are 'foreign', not our sort of people, which is why the cultural diversity that results from the internal fragmentation of society is so much more threatening than that which comes from outside. When it is our own people – our neighbours, friends, and relatives – who disagree with us, it is less easy to dismiss their views as being of no account. In that situation we are much more likely to change the status and the reach we accord our views. Of course, dogmatism is still common, but, especially as they are expressed in such public forums as the mass media, ideas and beliefs are often handled in a manner that, even if it is not consciously seen in these terms, is in practice relativistic. We handle our failure to agree by supposing that what works for you may not work for me, and vice versa. Values become personalized.

More will be said about relativism in the final chapter. Here I will summarize by saying that the rise of egalitarian individualism has consequences both for the organization of society (in essence increased freedom in private and increased constraint in public) and for the status we accord our ideas and values.

Anomie and social order

This is a slightly contrived link, but I would like to return to the nature of social order and the causes of crime, and the topic of egalitarianism does feature in what follows. Consider India. Here we have a country with extremes of wealth and poverty. Yet, compared to the United States, there is little crime and comparatively little of the vices we associate with urban social malaise: alcoholism, drug addiction, and suicide.

The core of the explanation is simple and was given in the 1950s by Robert Merton, who took Durkheim's arguments about the link between individual stability and social order and added a radical twist. It is often supposed that the crucial tension in social life is between the individual and the society. Crime and other forms of malaise result from a society insufficiently imposing its values on the minds of its members. Anti-social behaviour results from a lack of socialization. Merton took the rather different view that a tendency to crime and deviance was actually endemic to the modern society.

Naturally, this summary simplifies, but Merton's case was that we can understand a society as two relatively autonomous spheres: culture and social structure. Culture tells us two sorts of things: what we should desire and how we should behave. Structure describes the allocation of power, wealth, and status. The social structures of traditional societies are hierarchical. Some people are rich and powerful; most are impotent and poor. The culture reflects that disparity. Different groups of people are taught to expect very different things from life and to behave in ways appropriate to their station. So what people expect and what they get are in balance. The poor expect to be poor. Hence they accept being poor. In medieval Europe and in Hindu India this profoundly discriminatory system was legitimated by a widely shared religion that promised great rewards in the next life to those who humbly accepted their position in this life. The meek Christian expects to inherit the earth in the next life so long as he does not try to steal it in this. The poor but pious Hindu will be rewarded with a better birth in his next reincarnation.

What puts conflict right at the heart of the modern social system is that culture and social structure are no longer in harmony. The culture is democratic: the goals of material success are offered equally to everyone. The American dream promises that anyone can become President of the United States or at least president of a major corporation. As Andrew Carnegie put it: 'Be a king in your dreams. Say to yourself "My place is at the top."' Merton goes further and suggests that the United States (and here it may differ in degree from many European societies) makes ambition patriotic.

But equality of aspiration is not matched by equality of opportunity. The rhetoric of meritocracy encourages everyone to want the same things, but the reality of a class structure means that many people are denied the chance to attain their goals legitimately. As the social structure does not permit them to remain equally committed to the socially approved goals and to the socially approved means, they must lose faith in one (or both) parts of the value system. Merton suggests that there are five basic ways for individuals to adapt to the tension between goals and means.

Merton's typology of modes of individual adaptation.

Type of adaptation	Culture goals	Institutionalized means
I Conformity	+	+
II Innovation	+	−
III Ritualism	−	+
IV Retreatism	−	−
V Rebellion	+/−	+/−

To the extent that a society is stable, then *conformity* will be the most common and widely diffused position. Most people are committed to the goals and to the rules that specify how one attains them. *Innovators* are committed to the end result but reject the procedural rules. The combination of the relentless emphasis on success and the uneven distribution of the means to achieve it allows many people to feel justified in finding new (and illegal) ways to get on. Denied a realistic chance to become president of General Motors, the young Italian instead aspires to become head of a Mafia family.

The third type of adaptation, *ritualism*, is interesting. The British social-history literature offers many studies of the almost obsessively 'respectable' lower-middle class, and the type is well explored in the early novels of George Orwell. Here we have those people who have no serious prospect of being successful in worldly terms (and indeed are suspicious of too much ambition: that is getting ideas above your station) but who are none the less terrified of falling back into the working class. Dress and language codes become an important device for drawing a clear line between the respectable and the rough. As Merton puts it: 'It is the perspective of the frightened employee, the zealously conformist bureaucrat in the teller's cage of the private banking enterprise or in the front office of the public works enterprise.'

The *retreatist* response is the least common. In this category fall some of the adaptive activities of 'psychotics, autists, pariahs, outcasts, vagrants, vagabonds, tramps, chronic drunkards and drug addicts'. These are people who have given up on goals and means, or, to use the Australian metaphor, 'gone walkabout'. Finally, Merton adds a fifth response. *Rebellion* describes the deliberately selective attitude to goals and means of those people who seek to replace the prevailing order by a new world in which merit, effort, and reward are brought into alignment.

As with many other classics of the sociological tradition, Merton's theory of anomie inspired a large body of research that confirmed some elements of the model but cast doubt on others. In particular, scholars have been critical of Merton's expectation that innovation will be most strongly associated with the working class. The idea that disillusionment with the unfairness of a class system will cause those most disadvantaged to seek to enrich themselves by robbery, burglary, theft, and mugging seems plausible, but why then do those who have every opportunity to do well honestly none the less want to do better dishonestly? Why do financiers fiddle their customers? Why do rich businessmen fiddle their taxes? Although Merton does discuss white-collar crime, his view from the 1950s now seem rather naïve. As journalists have become less deferential to the rich and powerful, we have learnt a great deal about the workings of power Élites. If we consider just recent American presidencies, we have the scandal of Richard Nixon approving of his officials illegally weakening his opponents' election campaigns and then covering up the crimes; we have Ronald Reagan approving illegal arms sales to provide funds for illegal guerrilla armies in Nicaragua; and we have the very fishy financial dealings of people very close to Bill Clinton. I will avoid the minefield of trying to compare the social costs of the crimes of the rich and the crimes of the poor by saying, minimally, that few of us now share Merton's confidence that innovation is particularly strongly associated with the working class.

None the less, Merton has captured a vital point about modern societies. At the heart of any stable world is a shared belief that things are mostly as they *should* be. There need not be a dominant ideology that justifies social arrangements in detail and to which everyone enthusiastically subscribes, but there does need to be some sort of moral sense that most people get their just deserts. The Hindu notion of karma achieves that perfectly. Because it is built on the principle of repeated reincarnation, it can suppose that, however unfair things look right now, the bad people with good lives must have been good in a previous incarnation. More than that, they will suffer a worse rebirth in the next life as punishment for their acts in this round. Though Christianity is less good at explaining why bad things happen to good people, it offers a restorative mechanism in the notions of heaven and hell. But modern societies are largely secular and our desire for social justice has to be satisfied in this material world.

The egalitarian impulse, which, I have argued, is a central feature of the modern world, challenges the manifest inequalities of life. So long as meritocracy remains more of an aspiration than a reality, those who are encouraged to want a slice of the action but feel themselves denied a fair break will have little compunction about taking what they feel is due to them. The American journalist Studs Terkel once suggested that the motto of the city of Chicago should be 'Where's Mine?'. Two observations may save Merton's theory from the problem of middle-class innovation. First, we can note that experiences and reactions can become diffused and adopted by others outside the social location that most pressingly experiences the frustrations Merton identifies. It may well be that the working class first or most severely appreciates the inequitable nature of the world, but disregard for the law can become widespread. Secondly, we can go back to Durkheim's argument about the boundless nature of human desires (see pp. 20–1). Someone who has everything can still want more, and a culture that puts great stress on worldly success while promoting the rights of the individual over the fate of the community encourages everyone, irrespective of their objective position, to feel relatively deprived.

Postmodernity?

Although scholars differ in the weight they give to different causes in the above account of modernization, there is widespread agreement that industrial societies are fundamentally unlike the agrarian societies that preceded them. For most of the twentieth century, there was a further argument about which features of our world were a consequence of industrialization and which were a feature of the *capitalist* form of economy in which our industrialization had taken shape. The class structures, gender relations, patterns of religious observation, and crime rates of capitalist democracies were compared with those of the Communist bloc states. The complete collapse of Communism in the 1980s ended those debates. The attempt to see which parts of our past were somehow 'essential' and which were accidental has now shifted to comparison between our past and the present development of Third World countries. It is, for example, now possible to understand better our own history when we see how the development of the nation state, representative politics, and industrialization proceed in the very different context of Singapore, Japan, Korea, and China. The existence of such comparators has certainly contributed to the decline of the confidence of Western sociologists of the 1950s who believed that the history of the West provided a universal template for modernization.

There has also been an important shift in depictions of the West as many scholars (interestingly often philosophers and social theorists rather than sociologists) have argued that, though the above account of modernization is reasonably accurate for the nineteenth and early twentieth centuries, we have now moved into another epoch: the *postmodern* world. Although there are many strands to 'postmodernism' (an art style before it became a social theory), the basic idea is that individual freedom has combined with increased geographical mobility and better communication to create a world in which 'consumers' select elements of culture from a global cafeteria. Economies based on the production and distribution of things have been superseded by economies based on the production and distribution of ideas and images. Idiosyncratic preference, taste, and choice have extended to the degree that it makes little sense to talk of social formations such as class. An obvious illustration can be found in the matter of accents. Before the 1970s there was a clear association in such societies as the British and American between a certain accent and social prestige. Mass-media broadcasters spoke in the accents of the upper classes. It used to be possible to guess the political party of a politician by accent. British Tories spoke like members of the royal family; Labour politicians spoke in the regional tones of the working class. Such typing is now vastly more difficult. Well-educated middle-class children listen to 'gangsta rap' and other musical styles associated with the black poor of the inner cities and borrow vocabulary and accent, as well as borrowing dress and posture styles.

In politics, it is no longer possible to 'read off' people's preferences from their position in the class structure. Instead we find a variety of consciously created interest groups: radical student movements, environmental movements, animal rights campaigns, gay rights groups, and women's groups.

The nation state has become impotent. The globalization of trade and finance has radically reduced the ability of states to control their economies. Modern digital technologies of communication have radically reduced the ability of states to control their citizens. States are becoming increasingly subordinate to supra-national entities such as the European Union.

Even the certainties of birth, sex, and death have been blown away by transplant and reproductive innovations. Genetic engineering has given us the power fundamentally to alter the biological bases of identity. We have now cloned a sheep. We will soon clone people. In the postmodern world, nothing is solid. All is flux.

While there is something in such a description, it is grossly exaggerated. It is always useful to remind the intellectuals of London, Paris, and New York that much of the life in the provinces goes on little changed. Satellite TV might be a novel form of communication, but the soap operas we watch are little different from the novels of Dickens. Cheap international travel is now possible, but it takes as long to cross London now as it did when Sherlock Holmes solved the crimes of Victorian London. The heavy industries of the Ruhr and the Clyde have disappeared, but workers are still organized in trade unions and occupational class still affects people's attitudes, beliefs, and political behaviour. More significantly for the postmodern image of the autonomous consumer, the hard facts of people's lives, their health and longevity, remain heavily determined by class. To give just one example, at the start of the twentieth century working-class boys in London and Glasgow were on average 2.5 inches shorter than their middle-class counterparts. At the end of the century that is still the case. The popularity of divorce and remarriage has made the structure of the modern family more complex than that of its nineteenth- century predecessor, but the family remains the primary unit of reproduction and socialization and, for most of us, it remains a source of great satisfaction and psychic stability. While technological and social innovations have threatened the family, they have also provided resources for retaining the old habits in new times. Cheap high-speed travel allows us to be further away from each other, but it also allows us to regroup frequently. As we see when states limit trade, set quotas on immigration, and haggle over which will play what part in the 'international community's' response to this or that political crisis, the announcement of the passing of the nation state is, to say the least, premature.

It may well be that the modern societies that have preoccupied sociology were so dependent for their character on industrial manufacturing that a shift to an economy based on technological expertise and exchange will bring about such far-reaching changes to society and culture that we will at the start of the twenty-first century be justified in claiming a new epoch. But at present such designation seems premature and masks the fact that many of the changes heralded as 'post modern' are only extensions of the features of the modern world that fascinated Marx, Weber, and Durkheim.

Ironic consequences and social policy

In order to avoid repetition, one very important consequence of the ironic nature of social action has been held over to this point. The key sociological proposition that much of our world is inadvertent and unintended is important, not just for understanding why things do not go as planned but also for understanding why things are as they are. This has serious policy implications, because, if we misunderstand the causes of what concerns us, we misdirect our efforts to change it.

The point can be illustrated by considering the conservative critique of modern sexual liberality. Those who bemoan the decline of the 'traditional' family often blame the proportion of children in day care, juvenile pregnancies, high divorce rates, and, by extension, urban crime and juvenile delinquency on individuals or social-movement organizations that have openly championed easily available contraception, sexual liberation, easier divorce, and alternatives to the nuclear family. Liberal writers from the 'permissive society' of the 1960s are quoted and their opinions are taken to have been effective. That is, the problems are the result of deliberate policies advocated by these bad people. Hence the solutions are to restrain the opportunities for liberals to promote their ideals and for conservatives to become equally vocal in arguing the merits of traditional values.

However, a sociological approach to increasing divorce rates would suggest that, far from being the deliberate outcome of consciously desired ends, they are the *unintended consequences* of a large number of developments, many of them supported by and enjoyed by the conservatives who bemoan the consequences. Clearly much of the stability of marriage came from its role in allocating property and determining inheritance. When the bulk of resources took the form of heritable private capital, then determining just who was a legitimate heir was a vital matter. When there was a clear division of status so that the male was the head of the household and there was a gender division of roles, then there were good reasons to subordinate personal fulfilment to the stability of the family unit. But industrialization reduced the economic importance of the household as a unit of production and reduced the importance of 'legitimacy' (and with it many of the constraints on sexual activity). The development of contraceptive technology broke the link between sexual fulfilment and reproduction. Increasing individual affluence (and, for those who did not personally prosper, the creation of a welfare state) made it much easier for people not to band together in small units pooling resources and made it easier for us to dissolve those units when we no longer liked them.

Crucial also was the gradual expansion of the notion of egalitarianism. There were many legislative and political battles to be fought before the fundamental idea that all people were much of a muchness was translated into a culture of equal rights for all, but gradually rights were extended from landowners, to rich men, to not so rich men, to all men, and then to women.

The decline in the economic and political functions of the family allowed space for the development of a new justification for the nuclear family: the production of emotional satisfaction. In the 1950s American sociologists such as Talcott Parsons argued that the primary role of the family was to provide warmth and comfort and companionship. The family was to be a place where one recharged one's batteries and indulged in the personal and discriminatory behaviour that was increasingly outlawed in the public sphere. At work we were supposed to be rational and disciplined, to be confined by our roles, and to treat people on the basis of universalistic criteria. But at home we could relax and be ourselves. We could be honest. Worse than that, we were expected to be honest and open, which called into question the hypocrisy that had allowed our forebears to engage in extramarital activity while swearing lifelong fidelity. Concentration on psychological fulfilment places enormous strain on the institution because it raises impossibly high expectations.

A further complication comes from improvements in health. One of the most remarkable achievements of modern industrial capitalism is the increase in life expectancy. What is involved in swearing to love and cherish 'until death do you part' has changed dramatically since 1800 or even 1900. At the start of the twentieth century only 8 per cent of the British population was over 60 years old; by the end, it was over 20 per cent. It may seem a little callous to express it in these terms, but divorce can be seen as the modern equivalent of premature death.

The specific causal connections are complex, but I hope the above is enough to assure us that the decline of the traditional nuclear family had very little to do with the writings of the enemies of the family. Rather than being a cause, it is far more likely that such propaganda was a symptom of the changes already in progress. Changes in the family cannot be separated from changes in the structure of the economy, the expansion of the idea of rights, and increasing affluence. And those are all things that in the main the conservatives who bemoan the death of the family would not wish to have been otherwise.

The policy implication is this. When we concentrate on the individual person choosing a particular course of action, we risk the mistake of supposing that those actions will have the intended consequences. By overlooking the amply-evidenced fact that much action goes astray and that the world turns out as it does not because anyone wants it like that, but because actions engaged in for one purpose have unanticipated consequences, we risk exaggerating our own powers to engineer change. Especially if we can find some group of people who did want that change, we can readily (but mistakenly) suppose it happened because they wanted it and it can be reversed by us wanting something different.

The most florid example of this mistake is the conspiracy theory. The understandable desire to understand the world has lead to a huge and persistent market for simple theories of powerful hidden agents. So the Second World War was not the outcome of a very large number of actions engaged in by a very large number of individuals, groups, and organizations with very different goals; it was caused by the Jews, or the Freemasons, or International Communism, or some other unitary actor. If no this-worldly agent of sufficient potency can be imagined, then one can always invoke aliens. Such conspiracy thinking is actually a misdirected partial understanding of social causation. It rightly supposes that there is more to life than meets the eye and reflects the sense of the powerless that there is an order that is not immediately observable to the untrained eye. But then it reverts to the idea that things occur because someone wanted them like that. It fails to understand unintended consequences and the supra-individual causes of action.

Chapter 5
The Impostors

The previous chapters have tried to give some idea of the themes of sociology and the distinctive flavour of the sociological vision of the world. In order to clarify further that vision, this chapter will look briefly at various impostors in the sociology camp and then attempt a summary description of the discipline.

Improvers and utopians

There is an impression, widespread among our detractors and not unknown within the discipline, that sociology is (or should be) in the business of helping people. This is understandable but it is mistaken. It is understandable because many of the early contributors to the discipline were moved to their studies by a desire to alter the world. Karl Marx was primarily a revolutionary who wished to see unjust and oppressive capitalism replaced by a more humane economic and political structure. Such founders of the British tradition of empirical social research as Seebohm Rowntree and Charles Booth documented poverty because they hoped to shock governments into doing something about it. Sociology in Britain owed a great deal to the London School of Economics, and the close association of that institution with the Webbs (who founded the Fabian Society and were an influence on the early Labour Party) gave much of its work a clearly reformist tone. Some of the founding faculty of the University of

Chicago's Sociology Department had been raised in Protestant clergy families, and, though far from being Marxists, they would have heartily agreed with Marx that the point of studying the world was to change it.

However, though the discipline owes much to reformers and many sociologists derive their research interests from moral and political engagement with the world, sociology must be distinguished from social reform. An academic discipline can function only if it is driven by its own concerns and not those of others. Even the most confident advocates of the scientific method recognize the constant interplay of explanation and observation. We need tentative theories before we can know what to observe or how to describe it. For sociologists to collaborate in accumulating a body of knowledge, they need to speak a common language. For example, the comparative class analysis mentioned in the previous chapter is possible only because scholars in different countries use the same models. Furthermore, debates (for example, over the relative merits of Marxist and Weberian views of class) can be rationally advanced only if both sides agree to deal in the same currency. For this reason, only those ideas that are necessary to the task in hand should be allowed to guide our work.

That is easier to say than to ensure. The core ideas of genetics and of Soviet communist philosophy are sufficiently different for us to see their mixing in the Lysenko example as detrimental and distorting intrusion. But the study of social life and the reform of society share concepts, measures, and theories and that makes it especially difficult to avoid contamination. None the less, that has to be our aim. Productive dialogue between sociologists is best served by them making every effort to distinguish between the values necessary to the discipline (such as honesty, clarity, and diligence) and extra-disciplinary concerns that should be laid to one side.

Those of us who teach sociology routinely see the difficulty our students have in distinguishing between a social and a sociological problem.

When asked to choose a topic for their research projects, students almost invariably focus on something bad about the world. They want to 'do something about' the homeless or alcoholism or domestic violence, and the flaccid verb 'to do' is a clear symptom of the confusion between explaining and rectifying.

One way of clarifying the difference is to describe a sociological case study of some feature of the social world that might be widely seen as unacceptable. David Sudnow examined 'plea bargaining' in a California court. Some 80 per cent of cases never come to trial because the defendant agrees to plead guilty, which saves the courts a lot of money. To encourage the defendant to 'cop a plea', some reduction in the charge is usually offered. The supposed perpetrator is given a choice between contesting the case and risking a certain level of punishment or accepting as certain a lower level of punishment.

The California legal code recognizes the notion of a lesser offence. If in committing crime A, a person must also commit crime B and B gets a shorter custodial sentence, then B is the lesser offence. For example, robbery necessarily includes petty theft in the sense that one cannot rob without also committing petty theft. The procedures of the court specify that one cannot charge a person with two or more crimes, one of which is necessarily included in the other. For example, a person cannot be charged with 'homicide' and with the necessarily included lesser offence of 'intent to commit a murder'. The rules also say that the judge cannot instruct a jury to consider, as alternative crimes of which to find the defendant guilty, offences that are not necessarily included in the charged crimes.

Sudnow explains the legal principles governing charges and lesser offences because he wants to make a contrast between the formal rules and what actually happens. For the District Attorney (prosecuting) and the Public Defender (hereafter DA and PD), the interest in charging is quite different from the concerns enshrined in the legal codes. Rather than being concerned with what crimes were actually committed and the procedural rules about inclusion, they are concerned to strike a bargain. In order to persuade the defendant to enter a guilty plea, they need to find a lesser offence that carries a sentence sufficiently lower to seem like a good deal but not so much lower that the DA will feel that the defendant has 'got away with it'.

What Sudnow discovered was that offences were routinely reduced to others that were neither necessarily included nor actually included in the particular commission of the major offence. For example, 'drunkenness' was often reduced to 'disturbing the peace', even if the peace had not actually been disturbed. 'Molesting a minor' was often reduced to 'loitering around a schoolyard', even when the offence had taken place nowhere near a schoolyard. Furthermore, reductions often defied the nature of the original charge. Burglary was often reduced to petty theft, even though petty theft is necessarily included in robbery and robbery is clearly distinguished in law from burglary. Were one to take the legal code seriously, such a reduction would be a nonsense, yet it was routinely used. Why the DA and PD colluded in this defiance of the law is obvious: producing the right outcome was much more important than following the letter of the law.

But how was this practical goal achieved? The answer is that, through lengthy experience, the PD and DA had come to develop knowledge of the typical manner in which offences of given classes are committed, the social characteristics of the persons who regularly commit them, the features of the settings in which they occur, the types of victims often involved, and the like. They had built up a notion of 'normal crimes' based on intensive knowledge of their areas. Over a history of plea bargaining the two sides had developed recipes for successful reductions. Typical 'assaults with a deadly weapon' were reduced to simple assault, 'molesting' to 'loitering around a schoolyard', and so on. Although the recipes were applied to individual defendants, the particularities of each case were of little concern *provided the offence fitted into a typical box*. It was the class of offence and the typical class of offender that were at issue and the charge sheets were written up in such a way as to guide everyone involved to the correct interpretation. So the harassed defence lawyer, who might typically have only a few minutes to review the case, could quickly see what was required and what would work.

It would be possible to read Sudnow's work as a report on a 'social' problem. The cut-price justice that the system offered could be construed as a major infringement of civil liberties: people are routinely pressed into pleading guilty to crimes that nobody thinks they committed. However, none of that is Sudnow's concern. What he wants to know is not whether the justice routinely doled out by the courts is good or bad, but what it is and how it happens. His point is not to highlight the thing that needs correcting, but to identify the thing that needs explaining. In so doing he offers a well-documented example of the common phenomenon of people developing shared *ad hoc* typifications that they use to order the raw material for their work in a way that allows them to 'get on with the job'.

A similar theme informed the research of a postgraduate student who was a contemporary of mine at the University of Stirling in the 1970s. She wanted to understand the practical organization of psychiatric nursing and for a number of months she worked 'undercover' in a major Scottish mental institution. She quickly discovered that patients were managed within two quite different frameworks. The consultants classified patients according to formal diagnostic schema and prescribed treatment appropriate to the diagnostic categories. But the nurses, who were responsible for the day-to-day management of the wards, had a much simpler system that reflected their working concerns. They labelled patients as 'wetters' and 'wanderers'. The primary problem with the former was their incontinence; with the latter it was their lack of orientation. The nurses knew that their classificatory system would offend the consultants and the family and friends of the patients, so those terms were used only in private talk between nurses and in the 'backstage areas' such as the tea-room, the canteen, and the nurses' home.

Like Dalton's work on the disjuncture between formal models of organization and the informal organization of the workplace, these examples could be seen as identifying problems, and no doubt particular interest groups will wish to complain about them. But that cannot be a central concern for the sociologist. In setting their agenda, sociologists must be driven by what is sociologically interesting, not what is socially problematic. Erving Goffman's influential work on roles was built on the study of mundane everyday actions, not on the exotic or the especially troublesome. Howard Becker's labelling theory of deviance was the result of what, at the time and from the standpoint of a social reformer, might have seemed like a curious choice of topic. Why study marijuana-smoking jazz musicians when there is serious crime to investigate?

Agendas external to the discipline are an unhelpful distraction. Had Goffman viewed the mental institutions that provided much of the material for *Asylums* with the perceptions of either the psychiatrists or their critics, he might not have seen the sociological gold dust. Goffman takes a wide variety of trivial and previously unremarked bits of behaviour (such as using crayons as lipstick) and shows that they share a common and important social function: they are devices that patients use to maintain a sense of self-identity in a setting that was designed, for therapeutic purposes, to undermine it. Goffman finds the new meaning in what he observes because he approaches the field as a sociologist. Instead of seeing boarding schools, asylums, monasteries, and army training camps as unrelated places that should be seen as respectively educational, therapeutic, religious, and military, Goffman perceives that they have common sociological features that he expresses through the notion of a 'total institution'. Because he was thinking sociologically, Goffman asked questions of his data that others with different agendas and interests would not have asked.

Partisanship

The social sciences are particular vulnerable to betrayal of principle because a central premise – one of the strands of the charm bracelet – can, if misunderstood, provide a warrant for partisanship. When we recognize that reality is a human product, a social construction, we weaken the solid link between perception and objective reality and call into question the standing of our own accounts and explanations. We then go further and point out that how people see things owes a lot to their shared interests.

This is not a claim about honesty (though it can be closely related); it is about something more subtle than lying. What distinguishes ideology from dissembling is that ideologists believe. When conservative Christians in the United States claim (let us assume mistakenly) that the high level of teenage pregnancy is a result of atheists banning prayer from public schools, they are not lying. They are being influenced by their shared beliefs into seeing the world in a particular way. When entrepreneurs argue that the extension of labour rights will cost jobs, they are not dissembling. They are giving voice to views they sincerely hold, which happen to coincide with their material interests.

The natural temptation is to see our own views as accurate and the views of others as ideology, but sociology makes that difficult by identifying ideological influences in an ever-greater number of social groups. Two examples come particularly close to home. In the 1950s it was common to distinguish professions from other kinds of work by noting that doctors and lawyers, for example, experienced lengthy periods of training in which they acquired expertise, were free from external regulation (only a doctor is able to judge if a colleague has been negligent), could restrict entry to the profession, and enjoyed high levels of reward. A firm line was drawn between the professions and other forms of skilled labour (such as craft engineering) that also tried to limit access and thus improve rewards. When the professions did this, it was justified because they served some higher social good (health and justice). When engineers did it, it was an unwarranted restraint on trade, and in many countries it was outlawed.

Sociological studies quickly punctured the inflated self-image of professionals by showing that, although their advantages were real enough, the justifications offered for them were largely self-serving rhetoric. The lengthy training periods often had more to do with excluding those of the wrong class, race, and gender than with the acquiring of necessary skills. Professional self-regulation had more to do with hiding bad practice from lay scrutiny than with the social good. Professionals seemed as greedy and acquisitive as any other group of workers.

The pretensions of science were also deflated by sociological research that showed that scientists were extremely reluctant to expose their theories to refutation, that the social influence of cliques had a major effect on how new ideas were received, and that there were often no observable differences between the conduct of orthodox and pseudo-science. Far from having a method that guaranteed authority for its results, science looked pretty much like other forms of work. In the first chapter I explained why I think this downgrading of science is grossly exaggerated, but it has become popular in Western social science.

If sociologists undermine the special status of the professions and the sciences, where does that leave their own work? Does it not follow that the *profession* of social *science* is itself pervaded by ideology? Even if the discipline has no special ideological interests, most of its practitioners would be influenced by the general racial, gender, and class interests of the white, male bourgeoisie.

One seductive resolution to this conundrum is to abandon all pretence to scientific neutrality. As conventional scholarship provides no way of arbitrating between competing visions, we should take sides on grounds derived from outside the discipline and opt for the fully committed partisan vision. Goals such as accuracy are then replaced by an interest in the consequences of ideas, what Marx called *praxis*. What matters is not whether an explanation of crime, for example, is coherent and well supported by the available evidence (because plausibility and status as evidence are themselves ideological products), but whether a theory will promote the interests of whatever social group one supports. One brattish criminologist, who had himself made little contribution to the subject, preposterously questioned the work of one of the doyens of American criminology by rhetorically asking what Edwin Sutherland had ever done to promote popular struggles!

Another defence for the scholar as partisan has become popular in the areas of ethnic studies and women's studies. The claim here is not that objectivity is impossible; it is that, even if it were possible, it would hinder the sociological enterprise. In order to explain we must understand. In order to understand we must experience. Only a black person can really understand what it means to be black. Only a woman can understand other women.

One good reason to be suspicious of this argument is that it is not offered even-handedly. We do not find sociologists arguing that only aristocrats can usefully study the aristocracy or that only fascists can study fascism. Such special pleading is offered only by people on their own behalf. Often it has the appearance of being a lazy way of asserting (rather than demonstrating) the superiority of their claims. Clearly, possessing some trait may be useful in understanding others with the same characteristic. I made that point in my general defence of sociology in the first chapter. However, there can be no room in honest scholarship for trump cards.

The idea that one has to belong in order to understand is often made further suspect by the way in which the group to which one should belong is defined. In drawing a line between insiders and outsiders, we have to impute to the group a patently exaggerated (if not downright false) set of common experiences and interests. Obviously, not all women or members of ethnic groups share the same experiences or hold the same values. Margaret Thatcher may have been Britain's first woman Prime Minister, but she was remarkably unsympathetic to what feminists defined as women's interests. Colin Powell was the most senior black person in the United States armed services in the early 1990s, but he served under Ronald Reagan, the most conservative president of the twentieth century, and rarely associated himself with racial-minority causes. One response of the partisan intellectual is to expel such people from the honoured group: Thatcher was not really a woman and Powell was an 'Uncle Tom'. The other response is to substitute for the opinions of the real group what that group would have thought had its thinking not been distorted by ideology. The partisans of gender and race assert what their client group should have thought and then claim that as the vantage point from which the world should be viewed.

In defence of value neutrality

At this point I would like to offer a defence of the ambition of objectivity. The partisans argue that objective social science is impossible because sociologists cannot transcend their own ideologically constrained world-views. If this point is not a statement of faith, it must be treated as a testable proposition. With only a little flippancy, I would note first that the partisans themselves refute their case: ideology blinds others, but they have managed to see above the mists. Unless the partisans can provide a plausible and testable explanation of why they are immune to a disease that infects everyone else, their intellectual good health offers a good reason to doubt the prevalence and severity of the ailment from which the rest of us are supposed to suffer.

A second response is to note that, even if the ideology problem is real in the abstract, it may not be relevant for a lot of sociological research. To continue with the sickness and health metaphor, the illness might not impair all functions equally. To take the example of my own work on loyalist paramilitaries, the facts that I am Scottish rather than Irish and have little personal sympathy for nationalism may bear on some aspects of my studies but have no effect at all on others. To return to the case mentioned in the first chapter, I do not see how any ideological interests would give me a particular slant on the question of how terrorists attain leadership positions.

The argument against objectivity supposes that contaminating bias will distort all one's work. My own experience suggests that many interesting and important questions in sociology simply do not carry the sort of moral, ethical, or political charge that would cause differences in observation and explanation to vary systematically with the social interests of those studying such questions.

Yet, even when they do, we still find sociologists taking up positions that do not appear to have a regular connection with their interests. I offer an example from the sociology of religion. Some sociologists believe that religion has declined markedly in the modern world; others believe that behind the apparent decline is an enduring and fairly constant religiosity. Many sociologists of religion are themselves religious people and have been drawn to the discipline in order better to understand their own faith. So we might expect that the personal values of these commentators would influence how they see the evidence. But the protagonists do not line up as we might expect. Among those who are persuaded by the evidence of secularization, we find two liberal atheists, a Lutheran who was an evangelical in his youth and is now in the mainstream, a former Methodist who is now an ordained Anglican, a conservative atheist who mourns the passing of moral orthodoxy, an official of a major US denomination, and a professor in a conservative Baptist college. Those who believe that modern societies are almost every bit as religious as pre-industrial ones show a similarly broad range of religious positions. Especially when I observe that some of these scholars have changed sides, and that many find quite plausible elements of the arguments presented by their opponents, I conclude that this field at least offers no support for the general claim that interests cannot be transcended. A similar case could be made from the field of political sociology. Again we have scholars studying aspects of the social world in which they are personally involved and again we find no easy match between competing explanations of voting behaviour, for example, and political preferences.

A further response to the partisans is to observe that the quality of a body of scholarship does not depend solely on the personal virtues of scholars. As I noted for natural science (see p. 4), the social organization of the enterprise is also relevant. Sociologists work in a competitive environment that allows the ready exchange of ideas and information. However blinkered I may be, there are others who are keen to prove me wrong. Objectivity does not depend on each of us being severally devoid of extra-disciplinary values; competition and collaboration neutralize the distorting effects of any one scholar's biases.

Finally, I would like to note that it is perfectly sensible to recognize that it is sometimes difficult to transcend one's own beliefs and values and still strive to overcome obstacles to objectivity. As the American anthropologist Clifford Geertz nicely put it, we know that it is impossible to create an entirely germ-free environment, but none the less most of us would rather have a heart operation in a modern operating theatre than in a sewer.

Relativism

If one response to the problem of ideology is partisanship, another is relativism, which brings me back to the subject of postmodernism. If reality is unknowable, if no objective and accurate account of the social world is possible, then we can do no more than endlessly manufacture partial descriptions of what the world looks like from this or that standpoint. And none of those descriptions is superior to any other. Again what we see here is a complex interaction between aspects of the world as described by sociologists and the way in which some sociologists see their work. Relativism has become particularly popular among disciplines such as media studies and cultural studies that lie on the fringe of sociology, but, like cancer, it has fed secondaries throughout the body of the discipline. Like cancer, it needs to be eradicated if the discipline is to survive.

We can readily understand why relativism is popular in cultural studies. Whether Austen is a better writer than Blyton and Constable a better painter than Picasso is largely a matter of taste. In most societies, the social hierarchy produces a hierarchy of tastes; one particular class decides what is good and bad art. In the Britain of the 1950s the expression 'I don't know much about art but I know what I like' was attributed by the smug to the ill-educated lower middle classes as a joke, a way of insulting their lack of expertise. In the 1990s it became an expression of high democratic principle. Attempts to preserve a 'canon' of good culture were seen as Élitist folly. To suggest that Austen was a better writer than Blyton came to be seen as snobbery. In many Western democracies (the United States, in particular) attacks on cultural hierarchies took on a particularly bitter tone as they were attacked, not just for class, but also for gender and racial bias. High culture was dismissed as the work of 'dead white males'. While we might have some sympathy with such criticisms in art and literature, they raise the awkward question of just where one draws the line between what is legitimately a matter of personal preference and what is a matter of fact. Those of us who believe in rational thought and the possibility of social science would draw a vital distinction by saying that we can accord everyone the right to believe what they wish and yet still assert that some beliefs are wrong. I fully support the right of people to believe that the world is run by a conspiracy of international Jewish financiers or that the governments of the West are in regular contact with aliens, but I would insist that such beliefs are not well founded.

What the relativist does is expand the area of knowledge that should be seen as matters of personal preference and hence of legitimate disagreement. The democracy of civil rights becomes a democracy of knowledge and that takes the form of supposing, not that everyone has an equal right of access to knowledge, but that what everyone believes is equally likely to be true.

The case against relativism

Part of the appeal of relativism lies in its starkness. It is dramatic and clear, whereas the responses often seem mundane and unfocused. Fortunately, that does not stop them being good responses. They will not satisfy those who want simple and arresting formulas, but together they do form a comprehensive refutation of relativism.

One reply was briefly given in the discussion of the claim that class is no longer significant: research consistently shows otherwise. Now it is always possible to argue that this or that pattern of regularities is merely a product of the strategies used to find it. After all, the Zande chicken-poisoning witch doctor would assert that his theories of causation are amply supported by the evidence. But where large numbers of scholars from disparate backgrounds come to the same conclusions, it becomes less easy to suppose that their findings are some sort of collective delusion and more easy to suppose that they are actually making contact with some external realities. That our observations can be persuasive for scholars from a wide variety of cultures suggests that there is a real world out there, which is independent of our beliefs about it, and hence that we can at least aspire to making discoveries about that world that are more than just an expression of our beliefs and preferences.

The point about understanding across cultural and social boundaries is important. If postmodernists are right that no reading, no account, can have any greater validity than any other, then cross-cultural communication would be impossible. The whole notion of translation supposes that we can (at least in theory) distinguish between more and less correct translations. In any particular case, it may not be easy, but the fact (and it is a 'fact') that nation states negotiate treaties, that religious missionaries translate their sacred scriptures into foreign languages, and that, every day, millions of us successfully communicate across class, gender, racial, ethnic, and linguistic borders should be enough to persuade us that the relativist's pessimism is misplaced.

Translation is possible because, for all the anthropological variation, there is much that is common in human experience. One culture may have a strong preference for male offspring while another may treat baby boys and girls alike, but the joys and trials of parenthood are similar the world over. Cultures may differ in the way they like their beef. We used to value fat cattle, now we prefer lean meat. But it is precisely because cattle rearers the world over speak 'the same language' that they can compare the relative merits of lean over fat. For centuries the Masai of East Africa have raised cattle in the most hostile environments and one might suppose that they had little in common with the rich beef farmers of the north-east of Scotland, but the first pedigree herd of Simmental cattle in Africa was founded in 1990 as a result of a collaboration between the Masai and a farmer from Methlick, a small village in Banffshire. They were worlds apart, but they had a common love for cattle and could find a common language for common action.

The difficulty with this sort of rejoinder to relativism is that relativists can refuse to be impressed because they reject the rules of engagement. Like the partisan who dismisses every criticism as mere ideology, the relativist can assert that the very idea of subjecting the claims of relativism to empirical test is based on an approach to knowledge that relativism shows to be mistaken.

The best answer to such blanket refusal to come to terms is to ask if relativists act consistently on their avowed philosophical position. Clearly they do not. Postmodernists write books and lecture; they try to communicate their claims to others. They do so because they believe that they are right and others are wrong. If they took a full-strength dose of their own medicine, they would shut up shop. If no reading is superior to any other, then why destroy trees to announce that to the world? If it is not possible to distinguish truth from error, why do postmodernists argue with those who do not share their views?

Conclusion

In this short essay it would have been impossible to describe sociology by comprehensively listing the impressive contributions to our understanding of the world that have been produced by the discipline's practitioners. I have tried to make some reference to the major figures and their most significant contributions: Marx and Weber on class; Weber on rationality; Durkheim on anomie; Gehlen on instincts; Merton on the structural causes of crime; Mead and Cooley on socialization; Michels on oligarchy; Parsons on the family; Becker on labelling; and Goffman on roles and total institutions. I have also tried to include enough references to specific sociological studies to give some idea of what sociologists do. However, the text has been designed to present, not a summary, but a sense of sociology.

If sociology is to be anything more than interesting (and not always that interesting) speculation, it has to be *empirical*. That is, its theories and explanations must be based on sound observations of the real world.

Hence my selection of great names has leant towards those who have combined theory with detailed empirical studies. If it is to be empirical, then sociology must model itself on the natural sciences.

However, in asserting that sociology must be a social science, we must also bear in mind the peculiar disadvantages and advantages that come from the discipline's odd subject matter: we study ourselves. The capacities of reasoning and interpreting that allow us to do more than merely act out our instincts or respond to our physical environment are what allow us to study anything. In turn this means that we cannot hope to treat social action as the symptoms of underlying regularities akin to the laws of the physical world. We have to recognize the socially constructed nature of reality and study those social constructions (of which sociology is itself a particular systematized and refined example). To the partisan and the relativist this is a conundrum to which we can respond only by abandoning study and either taking sides on ideological grounds (the partisan view) or taking all sides or none (the relativist position).

As I have argued, both of these forms of surrender are an unnecessarily pessimistic response. It is certainly not easy to understand the causes of crime or the decline of religion in the West, nor to explain political preferences and educational attainment. But so long as, in our everyday lives, we continue to believe we can work out which buses go to the town centre, which churches offer to hear confessions, which political parties come closest to our preferences, and when our children are lying to us, I see no reason why we should believe that a more systematic examination of such questions on a larger scale is impossible. At various places in the text I have drawn attention to the ways in which sociological explanations differ from common sense: sociology recognizes the socially constructed nature of reality; it identifies the hidden causes of action; it describes the unanticipated consequences of action. But I would also assert that common sense itself provides the best warrant for the possibility of social science. Some of us are better at it than others and we all make mistakes, but everyday, in hundreds of small ways, we attempt to observe, describe, understand, and explain our actions and the actions of others. If we can do it as amateurs, I see no reason why, with greater effort, we cannot do it professionally.

Further Reading

In compiling the following I have tried to select books that are still in print, are regularly republished, or are likely to be available in most large libraries.

The best of the all-encompassing introductory texts is James Fulcher and John Scott, *Sociology* (Oxford: Oxford University Press, 1999).

The theoretical issues explored in Chapter 2 are dealt with in Peter L. Berger and Thomas Luckmann, *The Social Construction of Reality* (Harmondsworth: Penguin, 1976). It is in parts a difficult read and perhaps only for the truly dedicated. The main ideas appear in a briefer and more accessible form in Peter L. Berger, *Invitation to Sociology* (Harmondsworth: Penguin, 1990). The relationship between the individual and society also forms the main theme of Laurie Taylor and Stan Cohen, *Escape Attempts: The Theory and Practice of Resistance to Everyday Life* (London: Routledge, 1992).

The description of modern societies summarized in Chapter 4 owes a great deal to Ernest Gellner, *Plough, Sword and Book: The Structure of Human History* (London: Paladin, 1986), which, in under 300 pages and in admirably clear prose, explains the shifts from hunter-gatherer to agrarian to industrial societies. A. H. Halsey, *Changes in British Society: From 1900 to the Present Day* (Oxford: Oxford University Press, 1995), looks closely at the present state and recent history of one modern industrial society.

The classics are regularly reprinted, and, while Marx is both difficult and passé, Weber and Durkheim are still eminently readable. So I would recommend H. H. Gerth and C. Wright Mills (eds), *From Max Weber: Essays in Sociology* (London: Routledge, 1991), and Émile Durkheim, *Suicide: A Study in Sociology* (London: Routledge, 1970).

There are so many modern works that deserve to be classics that it is invidious to select just a few, but the following from the 1950s and 1960s combine acute observation and sociological reasoning to exemplify the best traditions of the discipline.

Becker, Howard, *Outsiders* (London: Free Press, 1963).

Dalton, Melville, *Men Who Manage: Fusions of Feeling and Theory in Administration* (London: John Wiley & Sons, 1959).

Goffman, Erving, *The Presentation of Self in Everyday Life* (Harmondsworth: Penguin, 1969).

Gouldner, Alvin, *Wildcat Strike* (London: Routledge & Kegan Paul, 1957).

Lockwood, David, *The Blackcoated Worker* (London: Allen & Unwin, 1958).

Young, Michael, and Willmott, Peter, *Family and Kinship in East London* (Harmondsworth: Penguin, 1961).

Since the 1960s the higher-education sector of all industrial societies has expanded massively, and with it the number of sociologists. The growth and increased specialization of the discipline have made it increasingly difficult for any studies to become known outside their particular field. The following are three books from the 1990s that show sociology at its creative best.

Devine, Fiona, *Social Class in America and Britain* (Edinburgh: Edinburgh University Press, 1997).

Foster, Janet, *Villains: Crime and Community in the Inner City* (London: Routledge, 1990).

Jamieson, Lynn, *Intimate Relations* (Cambridge: Polity, 1997).

Index

Sociology

Sociology

Index

Expand your collection of
VERY SHORT INTRODUCTIONS

Available now

Available soon

Visit the
VERY SHORT
INTRODUCTIONS
Web site

www.oup.co.uk/vsi

➤ **Information** about all published titles

➤ News of **forthcoming books**

➤ **Extracts** from the books, including titles
   not yet published

➤ **Reviews** and views

➤ **Links** to other **web sites** and main
   OUP web page

➤ Information about **VSIs in translation**

➤ **Contact** the editors

➤ **Order** other **VSIs** on-line